Plush You!

lovable misfit toys to sew and stuff

Kristen **Rask**

NORTH LIGHT BOOKS

Cincinnati, Ohio

12   11   10   09   08   5   4   3   2   1

Library of Congress Cataloging-in-Publication Data

Rask, Kristen.
   Plush You! : lovable misfit toys to sew and stuff / Kristen Rask.
       p. cm.
   Includes index.
   ISBN 978-1-58180-996-1 (hardcover : alk. paper)
   1. Soft toy making. I. Title.
TT174.3.R36 2007
745.592'4--dc22
                                    2007018482

Distributed in Canada by Fraser Direct
100 Armstrong Avenue
Georgetown, ON, Canada L7G 5S4
Tel: (905) 877-4411

Distributed in the U.K. and Europe by David & Charles
Brunel House, Newton Abbot, Devon, TQ12 4PU, England
Tel: (+44) 1626 323200, Fax: (+44) 1626 323319
E-mail: postmaster@davidandcharles.co.uk

Distributed in Australia by Capricorn Link
P.O. Box 704, South Windsor, NSW 2756 Australia
Tel: (02) 4577-3555

METRIC CONVERSION CHART

TO CONVERT	TO	MULTIPLY BY
Inches	Centimeters	2.54
Centimeters	Inches	0.4
Feet	Centimeters	30.5
Centimeters	Feet	0.03
Yards	Meters	0.9
Meters	Yards	1.1
Sq. Inches	Sq. Centimeters	6.45
Sq. Centimeters	Sq. Inches	0.16
Sq. Feet	Sq. Meters	0.09
Sq. Meters	Sq. Feet	10.8
Sq. Yards	Sq. Meters	0.8
Sq. Meters	Sq. Yards	1.2
Pounds	Kilograms	0.45
Kilograms	Pounds	2.2
Ounces	Grams	28.3
Grams	Ounces	0.035

F+W PUBLICATIONS, INC.
www.fwbookstore.com

Editors: Tonia Davenport and Robin M. Hampton
Designer: Cheryl Mathauer
Production Coordinator: Greg Nock
Photographer: J. Owens

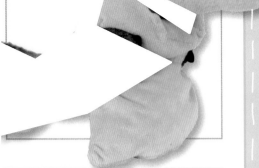

Acknowledgments

I'd like to thank a bunch of people for a bunch of things, but because there isn't enough room for all my thanks, I'll just thank these people:

Mom and Dad for everything—always. My sister, Chelsea; and brother-in-law, David: You're both really great. All the artists in this book for being so patient and nice. My editors, Tonia Davenport and Robin Hampton: I hope I didn't drive you crazy. Lisa Kious, you're the best friend anyone could ask for. Anna Links, you're the best and so dang helpful. Stuart Bloomfield for the foreword and being so fun to work with all the time. Vicky and Matt of Plexipixel: The logo designed by Matt is awesome. Yeasul Yoo, my intern. Joe Owens: Taking tons of photos has never been so fun. The Farukh family, Sally Brock, Erich Ginder, Lisa and Nate Burch, the Trent family, the Beard family, Cara Brooke, Zack Chambers, Maribel and Michael, Nelson Harst, the Depaz family (come back to Seattle now), Elena Moffet (I still want to clone you…please?), Barbara Pronsato, Nikki, Kate Greiner, Pamela Yearby (I love Tuesdays), Kori Clot, Betsy Nordlander, Frankie, Jackpot, Amos and all Plush You! supporters, volunteers and lovers.

May there be many more plush years ahead.

XO,
Schmancy

Contents

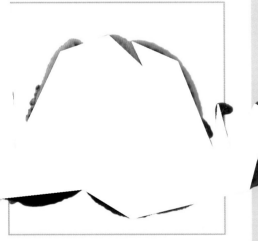

Plushie Projects

Plush Memories

—Stuart Bloomfield, a.k.a. Sewdorky

I remember my mom getting that thing out of the bottom of the beat-up cardboard box. It was so gaudy, so ugly—all gilt and lace—a chubby plush angel with rouged cheeks and wings made of doilies.

I was a sullen, suburban teen boy with a shock of Robert Smith-inspired hair and a fresh splash of Christmas-induced zits. The holidays were one of the few times of the year I'd voluntarily talk at home. "Y'aren't putting that thing on the top again, are you?" I asked.

"Stuff it, you. It's going on top," she chimed back as she climbed the step stool to reach the treetop.

"Man, I hate that thing. It's so lame. It's the epitome of suburban tackiness."

"Big words from such a morose mouth," she dished back. "Perhaps you better help before I talk Santa out of giving you that black eyeliner on your list, punk."

Even earlier than the angel incident, I remember my favorite plush animal, Hot Cereal. He was a sturdy little stuffed dog with brown ears and a mottled coat that reminded me of oatmeal. He'd been with me for as long as I had memories and was a friend I could always rely on—whisper kid secrets to and reach for late at night when woken from bad dreams and bumps in the dark.

He stuck around much longer than all my other childhood stuffed toys. He was the last to go, finally replaced by soccer jerseys, Star Wars action figures and Atari.

I also remember, wedged between these other two memories, the first time art dumbfounded me. It was my first encounter with Claes Oldenburg, who specializes in reinterpreting everyday objects as colossally oversized items. This one was a beaut, located in my Midwestern hometown museum. It was a gigantic electrical plug, stuffed and sewn of burgundy leather measuring at least 20 feet (6m) long and hung gloriously from the ceiling of a three-story atrium. For a ten-year-old geekboy like me, it was a brain revolution. I would visit it as often as I could, staring at it from all angles. Whatever else was in the museum always paled; this thing was awesome. This was art with a capital A. Someone made this! Genius!

❀❀❀

I dig up these memories when thinking about my continued love of all things plush. These were perhaps pieces of the puzzle that make my own view of art, craft, beauty, the world, whatever. For me, plush work isn't simply about the cute and cuddly. Plush is about nostalgia and comfort, but it's also about innovation and magic. Often plush art represents real-world things but in a surreal, softly perfect way.

The art of *Plush You!* proves my point. Not only cute and adorable—much of it certainly is—this is stuff to spark the imagination, to remind you of childhood, to comfort you in your darkened apartment, to make you smile in your cubicle or to simply make you wonder and dream.

It's also a collection meant to inspire you to create for yourself. Nothing here is too tough to do with just a little bit of know-how. That's another thing to love about plush: It's accessible not just from the end result ("Oh, look, it's a bear!") but also in its DIY execution (Anyone can do it!). There are tutorials to get the juices flowing and put ideas in your head. Take them and tweak them and come up with your own *Plush You!* marvel.

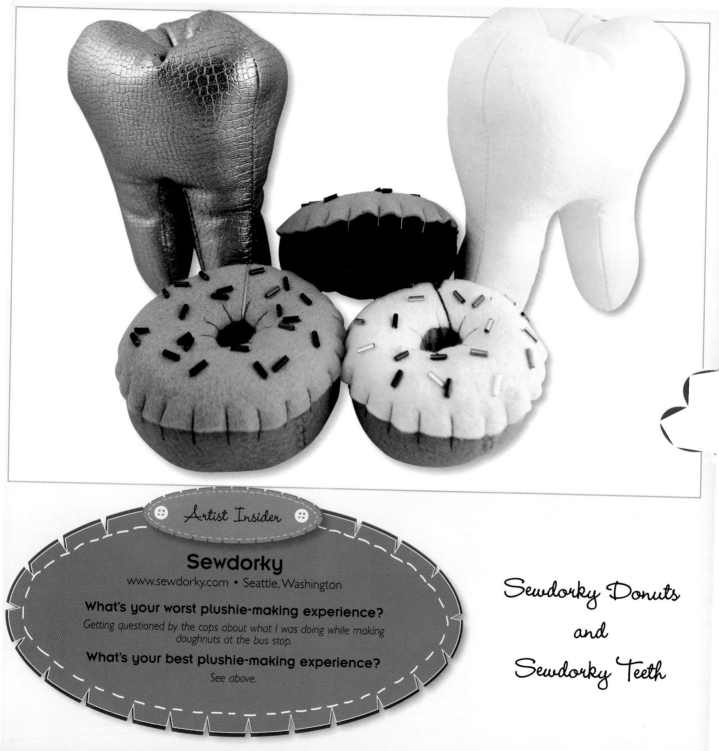

Sewdorky Donuts
and
Sewdorky Teeth

Editorial note: *Plush You!* is set up for you to browse like an art gallery and to learn the nuts and bolts of plushie making. Whether you decide to immediately dive into the gallery of more than one-hundred plushies or go directly to the Table of Contents (page 4) to find the tutorials, you're sure to find a plushie that inspires you.

I've been making stuff for as long as I can remember. I've realized, as I've gotten older, that creation is the one thing that seems natural and always a part of me. Being crafty has been my life source, friend, obsession, adrenaline rush, grace. When I was a kid, you couldn't have called me sporty or competitive, but I could sit and spend eight hours working on a piece of jewelry, deconstruct it and still feel satisfied.

In the summer of 1985, I had my first taste of making a living from my art. I was at camp, right on the cusp of my middle school years. I signed up for all the crafty classes, where I met two friends, Betsy and Leah. We began a small friendship-bracelet operation, accumulating thirteen dollars each to spend as we pleased. That was my catalyst for making things that I would then sell for some extra cash. Since then, I've made countless pieces of jewelry, purses, knitted items, pins, crocheted items, oven mitts, hairpins and button rings.

The button rings were a hit and paved the way for me to meet Sally at Fancy, a cute store in Seattle selling handmade items by many local and not-so-local designers. I found Sally's life enchanting. When the storefront next to Fancy became available, I signed the lease and opened a toy store called Schmancy before I had time to think about bills, overhead or cans of paint. Almost immediately, I began to take more risks and trust myself.

In addition to other crafts, I've had a long-standing love affair with plush. As a toddler, I dragged my first best friend, Raggedy Ann, around with me until her legs were made of masking tape, her head had a huge hole with the stuffing coming out and she was stained all over. I cared about her and took her anywhere I could. Now that I'm in my thirties, carrying a stuffed animal might be a little bit weird. However, I do have stuffed creatures hanging on my walls at home to serve as sources of inspiration. The plush movement for adults seems to spark imagination and creation. Since Sun-Min Kim and David Horvath created the Uglydolls in 2001, we've seen many other artists move into the plush medium. I love selling plush because it threads so many different people together. I have customers of different ages, economic statuses, interests, etc. This is what makes Schmancy special and what really started me thinking about *Plush You!*

In 2005, I created the Plush You! show at Schmancy to celebrate the work of plush artists from all over the world, including some of my favorite bloggers. I received tons of e-mails from strangers offering help and praise. The first show was a lot of work, but I'm used to work, and it turned out to be great fun. After the first year, I decided to make it even bigger. Sally volunteered her store, Fancy, so the Plush You! show could double in size. I'm continually amazed at the quality of the work submitted for the show and at the public's response to plush art. *Plush You!* is my way to combine my love for making things, my amazement at what others create and my love for the humble artists of the DIY movement. I'm delighted to showcase remarkable work made throughout the world, and I hope you enjoy what I've brought together. My hat's off to all you crafters who've made *Plush You!* my proudest work yet.

XO,
Kristen

Materials

So you're ready to begin plush makin'. Now you need some basic equipment to get started. Whether sewing is old hat for you or you're just discovering it, this book will help you find new ideas, inspiration and skills along the way. Here are some basic tools you'll need, along with some favorites from the artists. No matter what, have fun with your project, be creative and, most important, be yourself.

Fabric
Fabric is super fun to shop for because there's so darned much of it. There are tons of cool online fabric shops (see page 140) and surely at least one in your town with good sales and a good selection of basic fabrics. Thrift stores are a favorite place for *Plush You!* artists to find their fabric treasures at lower costs, too.

Thread
Thread is necessary but also fun as it comes in so many pretty colors. It's available in cotton, silk, embroidery, hand-quilting and invisible varieties, to name just a few. Denise Cozzitorto loves Sulky's invisible thread for sewing her plushies closed. Once you discover your favorite, it's the beginning of a long and beautiful relationship.

Scissors
Scissors are so important in your craft box. Good ones are even more important! I like to mark my sewing scissors so that no one uses them for paper or trimming bangs—or anything else for that matter. I can't live without my Gingher appliqué scissors. They're awesome for cutting small pieces of fabric, circles, etc. If I got a tattoo of scissors, it would be this pair…that's how much I love them. Invest in good fabric scissors; they're worth every penny.

Sewing Machine

You don't have to have a sewing machine, but it definitely helps your plush-making process go faster. Shawn Smith of Shawnimals loves his Singer model 1802. Other brands to consider: Bernina, Kenmore and Brother. Establish what you want from your machine and shop around. *Craft:* featured different artists' machines on its blog (www.craftzine.com) with information on each model. This is a great resource for a first-time buyer (or even a second-time one, for that matter). eBay might also be a great place to find a machine for less. Wherever you buy your machine, hunt for the best machine for your needs in your price range.

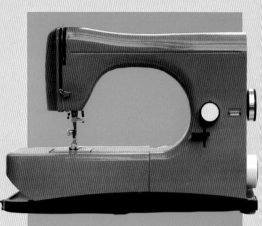

Sewing Needles and Pins

Whether you are hand sewing or machine sewing, you can't sew without these. Debbie Severtson loves her pins long, very thin and very sharp with a big plastic head. That sounds dirty! The best part about pins is that they, too, come in pretty colors. We're all about the cute and pretty.

Stuffing Material

Often called batting, your preference for stuffing material is another item you'll discover through trial and error. Everyone has his or her preference. It's available in cotton and wool, dense or fuzzy, etc. Some artists use polyester filling, while others use rice, beans, old shirts or plastic bags. You'll find your favorite in no time and never look back.

Pincushion

When I asked all our contributing artists to suggest some of their favorite tools, I was amused to find how many artists praised the virtues of a portable, adorable pincushion. Whether yours is cute or just functional, pincushions are essential to any crafter, pro or no.

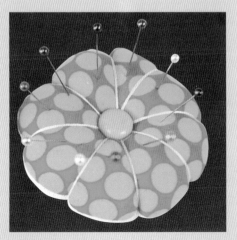

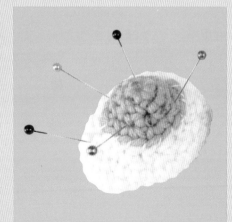

Sir Sulks-a-Lot

As you may (or may not) already know, I hail from the floating islands that hang just above the lumpy bumpy mountains. My generally caustic disposition is offset by my true nature, which, as those who know me will attest, is just a lot of fluff. I used to consume lots of hamburgers but have recently gone vegetarian. Like a stinky, grumpy old grandfather, I go about my business, which involves very little other than staring off into space and mumbling under my breath. (I really detest plain tofu.)

Necessities

canvas or muslin*

fabric marker

acrylic gesso

acrylic paint

chipboard or Davey board

polyester fill or supermarket bags

thread

bucket

paintbrushes

needle

scissors

sewing machine

*Canvas is great for painting on, but is harder to sew; muslin is easy to sew, but will soak up more paint.

Artist Insider

P. Williams
www.pwilliamsart.com • Seal Beach, California

What are your helpful hint(s) for aspiring plush artists?

Anyone can do it! I don't know anything about sewing, or even plush for that matter, except for a home-ec class I took in seventh grade where I made a pillow. I got an F in that class, no joke.

1 **Lay out fabric**

Fold fabric so you have 2 layers of fabric. [I don't restrict the size of any of my plush characters. I've made them from 1½" (4cm) tall to 7 feet (2m) tall.]

2 **Draw character**

Use a fabric marker to draw a rough shape of what you want your character to look like, or use my pattern (on page 138). (Fabric markers are more or less waterproof, and the ink won't leach through the paint you'll be covering the plush with later.)

3 **Add personality**

While drawing the shape, sketch the features you want it to have to give you an idea of the character's finished proportions. This also gives it a personality from the start.

4 **Cut fabric**

Cut 2 pieces of fabric about ½" (1cm) larger than your outline—one piece is for the front, the other for the back.

5 **Start sewing**

Use regular thread and set your sewing machine at 3m/m for straight sewing. Follow the line drawn on the fabric and leave about a 3" (8cm) section open on one of the bottom corners. (The opening may have to be larger or smaller depending upon the size of plushie you are making.)

6 **Cut notches**

In the seam allowance around the curved parts of the character, cut small Vs at ½" (1cm) intervals, pointing toward—but not too close—to your stitching. This makes for a nicer-looking shape and makes the excess fabric more pliable and less of a sculptural element.

7 **Turn material right-side out**

Now for the fun part: turning it right-side out. This is your first peek into what it's actually going to look like.

8 **Stuff plushie**

Using polyester filling (for thinner fabric) or even plastic bags (for heavier fabric, such as canvas), form your character. Pat it down occasionally to keep the fill from getting lumpy and to keep the distribution even.

9 **Add bottom**

When your plushie is as full as you want it, put a piece of chipboard or Davey board—cut to the size and shape you want the bottom to be—in the hole at the bottom. This allows the plushie to sit up a little better. Using a needle, thread and lots of concentration, stitch the bottom of the character, carefully folding and sewing down any excess fabric.

10 **Prime plushie**

Use gesso, an acrylic-based primer, to paint the plushie. I usually paint the top half first, leaving the bottom half unpainted. Let it dry as much as possible before sealing the bottom half with paint. I apply 2 to 4 coats of primer to unify the surface and give it more of a "shell" of paint.

11 **Paint plushie**

In a sealable container, mix acrylic paints to create the color you want the character to be. Be sure to mix extra to fix any mistakes. Cover the character with a solid coat of color. Once it's dry, paint on any features—lumps and bumps—that give it personality. (Mix a bit of the leftover body color with varying and increasing degrees of white paint to make highlights and accentuate the features you like.)

Artist Tip

I like using canvas because it's heavy and thick, and as a painter I've grown accustomed to its weight and tactile qualities. But it can destroy sewing-machine needles if, like me, you don't really know much about sewing. Also, its thickness can make hand stitching a real drag. So, I also use muslin. Just about any fabric can work: old T-shirts, bedsheets, whatever you have lying around.

Cupcake
Bears

Artist Insider

Amigurumi Kingdom by Jou Ling Yee

www.amigurumikingdom.com • Elmhurst, New York

What's your favorite extracurricular activity?
Sleeping.

Lil' Dickie

Artist Insider

John Black
Seattle, Washington

What's your favorite sandwich?
Chachi's Favorite at the Honey Hole in Seattle.

15

Burds

Artist Insider

BURD by Lucy Marten

www.hellobabyburd.blogspot.com • Staten Island, New York

Why do you do this?

I started making Burds when I got pregnant. A bunch of friends of mine were also pregnant, and I wanted to make them something special for their babies' rooms.

Pollyhams

Minouchka,
Minouchki and
Minouchka

Artist Insider

Beth Doherty
www.gourmetamigurumi.com • Chicago, Illinois

What's your favorite brain food?
Coffee, duh!

Amigurumi
Dolls

Woollyhoodwinks

We're Gamin, Chulo and Vinca, the cousins of the Woollyhoodwinks, though we've never actually visited the Black North Forest. The spirit and spunk of the our cousins courses freely through our fibers. We're always scheming up new and brilliant ways to entertain each other…and you! We love everything playful and fun, have boundless energy and can be seen galavanting over hill and dale, leaving giddy trails of harmless pranks and half-eaten berries in our wake. We fall in love with each day, and are sure the feeling is mutual. But as the shadows grow longer, to where do we three retire? There are many theories, but no one knows for sure.

Artist Insider

Woollyhoodwinks

www.woollyhoodwinks.com • San Francisco, California

1 Cut 2 of each pattern

Trace and cut 2 of each pattern piece (on page 134). Use the solid fabric for pieces A (head) and C (legs). Use the complementary fabric for B (body) pieces.

2 Form body

Sew 1 piece A (head) and 1 piece B (body) together to form the front panel of the plushie. Iron the seams flat. Repeat to form the back panel.

3 Fold C pieces

Fold pieces C (legs) in half lengthwise and sew. Turn right-side out.

4 Create face

Take the front panel from Step 2 and use buttons and stitching to create the face you want your creature to have. When positioning the eyes and mouth, keep in mind that you'll lose a little on the sides and top of the head when you sew the back and front panels together.

5 Sew front and back pieces together

Lay the back and front pieces from Step 2 on a flat surface, right sides together. When lined up, place a couple of pins in the center of the body to hold the pieces in place. Sew the front and back together. Remove pins and turn the piece right-side out.

6 Stuff your plush

Stuff the legs to about half full. If you're using lentils, sew the legs shut just above the fill line, to keep the needle path clear. Stuff the body to about 1" (3cm) from full if using polyester filling.

7 Complete sewing

Fold in the bottom edge of the body, pinning one side, and stuff a leg up into the other side, pinning that into place. Remove the first pin, stuff the other leg into the body and immediately place it under the sewing-machine needle and sew straight across the bottom, sewing the legs in and body shut, removing any remaining pins as you go. Voilà!

Necessities

solid fabric

complementary fabric (plaid or tweed or herringbone for body. Old Pendleton shirts are perfect for this.)

buttons or doll eyes

embroidery thread for the mouth

stuffing material: lentils or polyester filling

iron

pins

scissors

sewing machine

Artist Tips

❊ This is a fast and easy pattern to create a cat or a monster or a cat-monster. The possibilities are limitless, as you can be very creative with the face.

❊ If you choose buttons for eyes, try placing small dark buttons on top of larger white ones for a livelier look. Small white buttons can also make interesting teeth.

❊ For a puffy, stand-straight-up creature, polyester filling works well. For a heavier, more "relaxed" creature, try stuffing with dry lentils, rice or popcorn.

Brown Recluse, Señor P. and Moodzilla

Artist Insider

Blobby Farm

www.blobbyfarm.com • Colorado Springs, Colorado

Do you prefer cake or pie?

Cake. I've been studying cake decorating recently. So there's more cake in our house than we know what to do with.

Fuzzy
Monster

Artist Insider

Longoland
www.longoland.com • Brooklyn, New York

Do you have your own collection of toys and/or plush?
A few years ago Shawnimals (see page 96) and I traded originals on good faith—he is superific—otherwise, not really. I have several garbage bags of my own experiments that I won't let people see until I find a home for them. I just don't have room.

Modbird

Artist Insider

Lisa Congdon

www.lisacongdon.com • San Francisco, California

What's your favorite sewing machine?

Right now I have a Janome. It's a rock star.

Mr. Beardsley as The Swede and The Granola Eater

Artist Insider

Laura Granlund
www.intimidnation.com • Chicago, Illinois

What are your goals for your plush business?
*To publish the story of Mr. Beardsley.
Don't you want to know where he came from?*

Mr. Snarly Pants

I love to dance in my leopard-skin pants. I can do a four-way-directional split like nobody's business. I like to call my signature move the "North South East West." When I'm feeling especially wild I even do it inverted with a head spin. Watch out for me on the dance floor because I'm outta sight! RRRROWR!

Necessities

- red super shaggy fur, 12" x 16" (30cm x 41cm)
- animal print fleece, 12" x 16" (30cm x 41cm)
- black felt, 5" (13cm) square
- white felt, 5" (13cm) square
- three 40mm googly eyes
- polyester stuffing
- black, white and red thread
- drawing utensil
- hot-glue gun
- hot glue
- pins
- scissors
- sewing machine

Artist Insider

Jenny Harada
www.jennyharada.com • Pickerington, Ohio

Do you have a helpful hint?

Don't forget your rulers!

Trace and cut pieces

1 Trace and cut the following pattern pieces (on page 138): 2 legs from the animal-print fleece; 3 eye sockets from the black felt; and 2 head pieces and 8 feet pieces from the red fur (keep your scissors close to the weave of the fabric to avoid cutting the long shaggy hair).

Sew teeth

2 Trace the teeth onto the top half of the white felt with something that won't show through to the other side. Don't cut out the teeth yet. Fold the white felt in half so the traced teeth are facing out. Load your sewing machine with white thread; stitch from the top corner of the teeth following the line you traced, around the bottom of the teeth and back up to the other top corner of the teeth. Backtack at the beginning and end of your stitch. Leave open the straight line at the top of the teeth.

Cut and form teeth

3 Cut straight across on the top line of the teeth. Leave ⅛" (3mm) around the sides and teeth. Snip straight across the bottom of the teeth to cut off the points and also snip into the three concave parts between the teeth. Be very careful not to cut any of the sewing you just did! Turn the teeth right-side out. Use something with a blunt point to help you get the points of the teeth turned. A dull, white pencil works well for this.

Form eyes

4 Pin the 3 eye sockets onto one of the head pieces. Leave room from the edges so you don't sew the eye sockets into the seams later. Sew on the eye sockets using black thread and a zigzag stitch.

Assemble plushie

5 Pin the feet onto the bottom of the legs, right sides together. Stitch together. Pin each head piece to a leg piece. Sandwich the teeth between the head piece with the eye sockets and the legs. Stitch the heads to the legs. Flatten the front and back of the body with right sides together, then pin all around the body, making sure the shaggy hair is tucked in. Stitch around the entire body, leaving a 2" (5cm) opening on one side of the legs, near the head. Backtack at the beginning and end of your stitch.

Stuff and finish

6 Snip in the corners between each leg. Be careful not to cut into your seam. Turn your plushie inside out through the leg opening. Lay your plushie flat and brush the hair away from the eye sockets. Use hot glue to attach the eyes to the eye sockets. Allow to cool completely. Stuff him with polyester filling. Sew up the hole using a ladder stitch and strong thread.

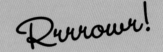

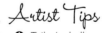

Artist Tips

❋ Tailor's chalk or a soft white pencil both work well for writing on black felt. A regular lead pencil works well for white felt.

❋ To avoid sewing hair into the seam, brush the red fur of the feet and the head pieces so that the hair along the straight line goes toward the center of the piece.

Wormies

Artist Insider

Madame Edgar
Montrèal, Canada

Is this your full-time job? If not, what is?

*I've owned a toy gallery/boutique for a year and
a half in Montrèal, Canada.*

Le Merde

www.lemerde.com • Seattle, Washington

What are your goals for your plush business?

For people to be "Vanderized."

Vander

Breaktime

Artist Insider

Ariana Marinelli

www.furrybanana.blogspot.com • Portland, Oregon

If you won the lottery, what would you buy for your plush/crafty business?

I would buy a studio space, and I would employ a studio assistant to help me so I could work faster!

Screenprinted Hamsters

Artist Insider

Jess Hutchison

www.jesshutch.com • San Francisco, California

What are your helpful hint(s) for aspiring plush artists?

Look through books and magazines (and the outside world!) specifically for color combinations that float your boat, and then take some crayons or colored pencils or paint and re-create them on a blank piece of paper with blocks of color. When you want to design a toy, look through these color combos for inspiration.

3

Oysters
and
Toaster

Super-Deluxe Quilted Sweater Socktopus

Artist Insider

Blackbird Fashion by Clarity Miller
www.blackbirdfashion.com • Anacortes, Washington
What do you listen to while you work on plush?
Laura Veirs, Bob Dylan, Joni Mitchell and audiobooks.

Stuffed Birds

We may be stuffed, but you won't find us gracing your Thanksgiving table. We'd rather throw on our aprons, grab a broom and help you get ready for guests. Just make sure the menu is strictly for the birds...all veggie.

Artist Insider

Cherry Tomato

www.cherrytomato.typepad.com/about.html • Seattle, Washington

What's your favorite fabric?

I couldn't possibly limit myself to one, but I adore cute Japanese fabric, natural linen and, of course, vintage fabric.

Necessities

wool felt—any color for body, bottom and feet

orange wool felt for beak

black wool felt for eyes

white wool felt for eyes

patterned cotton fabric for belly and wings

black embroidery floss

orange embroidery floss

embroidery floss to match belly fabric

stuffing material

pins

needle

scissors

sewing machine

rice or dried beans (optional)

4 **Stuff bird**
Turn the bird right-side out through the 2" (5cm) gap. Stuff the body—with polyester filling or other stuffing of your choice—through the open gap. To add stability to the bird, you can make a pouch filled with rice or dried beans and insert it in the bottom. When you're finished stuffing the bird, use a needle and thread and hand sew shut. Holding the gap closed, blind stitch the gap.

1 **Cut pattern pieces**
Cut out the pattern pieces (on page 137) as follows: 2 of the body, 1 of the bottom, 2 of the wing, 2 of the foot, 2 of the eye, 1 of the beak and 1 of the belly.

2 **Pin and sew pieces**
Take 1 piece of the body and lay it flat. Take both wings and pin them to the body. Place the second piece of the body on top and pin everything with right sides together. Sew the front and back of the body together with a ½" (1cm) seam allowance. Don't sew the straight edge of the body—it will be attached to the bottom of the bird. Trim the felt close to the seam around the top of the body. Remove the pins.

3 **Attach bottom**
Pin the bottom onto the sewn body. Carefully sew the bottom onto the body, leaving a ½" (1cm) seam allowance. Leave a 2" (5cm) gap for stuffing.

5 **Sew face**
Line up the eyes so they are evenly placed on the bird. Pin them into place. Using a needle and three strands of black embroidery floss, stitch the eyes onto the body using a blanket stitch. Attach the beak using a needle and three strands of orange embroidery floss by stitching across the middle of the beak. Fold the top and bottom of the beak shut. (It won't close all the way.)

6 **Attach belly and feet**
Using a needle and 3 strands of embroidery floss of your choice (something to match the fabric you have selected), blanket stitch the belly onto the body of the bird. Using 3 strands of the orange embroidery floss, attach the feet onto the bottom of the bird using cross-stitches. Embellish as you like—add tufts of hair, cheeks and accessories. You're finished! You now have a darling little bird.

Little

Fiends

Artist Insider

Chandra Rankin
www.littlefiends.com • Vancouver, British Columbia

What's the weirdest tool you use to create your plushies?
When I work on my miniatures, I use a chopstick to push the fill into tight corners.

Zombies

Magdalena Pereyra
Victoria, Australia

What's your favorite sewing machine?
My trusty sewing machine is a Brother 531 made in 1950 (I would guess). It weighs a ton.

37

Flapper Dolls #1 and #2

Artist Insider

Abby Glassenberg

www.whileshenaps.typepad.com • Wellesley, Massachusetts

Do you have your own collection of toys and/or plush?

No. Actually, I don't have any soft toys except the ones I make, and even then I try to sell them or swap them or give them as gifts as soon as they're made. I feel like once I've photographed them and blogged about them, they've been fully documented and are ready to travel out into the world. I really have no desire to own soft toys. I desire to make them.

Fifi Frog and
Sam Frog

Cannibal Bunnies: Embellish Your Plush

...with Blood and other Bodily Fluids

Dimensional paint is a great product that's used for a variety of craft purposes. Not to be confused with the ever-fun puff paint, dimensional paint is a thick, acrylic paint that doesn't lose "body" or its three-dimensionality when it's dry. It can be found most anywhere you find craft supplies. There are quite a few different manufacturers producing it in many consistencies and finishes, including shiny, glitter and pearl. (I use shiny; it helps make the blood look more real and fresh!)

40

Artist Insider

Serena Kuhl
www.flickr.com/photos/pocti • Northern Territory, Australia

Do you have a helpful hint?
I love to use my finger comb to pull fibers out of seams.

Gimp Bunny and Cannibal Bunny

Apply paint

1 Here we have a poor little bunny whose throat has been cut. Give him a bit of dimensional-paint goriness by adding a straight line of paint along the cut site. Don't be too picky about this; as you can see, dimensional paint tends to come out in blobby lines rather than smooth neat ones.

Add droplets

2 Create the illusion of blood by adding a series of running drops from the cut from Step 1. Create a blob of paint just below that line. Squeeze a bit of paint and touch it to the fabric to create a little pointy blob that looks a little like a chocolate drop. Hold the bottle there, not breaking contact with the paint, and increase the pressure to add more paint. The pointy blob will swell to a nice round shape. This technique makes blood, drool or whatever look as if gravity is at work and the fluids are pooling at the end of the drip. In other words, it looks more real. Without breaking contact, move away from the blob and draw your paint up until it rejoins the line you created before. Repeat for the desired number of droplets. (I apply the blood drips in one continuous motion, not individually, but I don't think it would matter if you did them separately.)

Allow time to dry

3 Finished! Now set it aside to dry. This can take up to eight hours. Don't touch it until it dries, as you could ruin the shine of your blood and blot paint all over your fabric. So lay your piece to dry away from pets, children and your own sleeves.

Artist Tip

It's important to cap the bottle after use, as it dries easily. Also, prepare the bottle before each use, whether it's a new or used bottle. A phenomenon I like to call "Dimensional Paint Flatulence" can occur if you don't shake the contents toward the tip with a couple of good downward motions. You should feel the paint settle in the top of the bottle. If you omit this step, air bubbles can interrupt the flow of paint when you apply it. Because you apply the paint by squeezing the bottle and touching the paint to the fabric like you would use an icing bag on a cake, if there are air bubbles you'll get a small explosion of air and fine bits of paint splattered all over your surface. I haven't been able to find a way to get paint, wet or dry, off fabric, so it pays to be careful. A good rule of thumb: Paint on a piece of paper first before you apply the paint to your project.

Now on to Other Bodily Fluids...

The same principal you use to make blood can be applied to other bodily fluids. If you've always wanted to make a plushie that's drooling with boredom, nauseated and vomiting, or picking its nose, you can do all this with dimensional paint. Reverting back to your inner five-year-old has never been so visceral!

Tears
To create a rueful toy, place small blobs of acrylic paint (in whatever color you think your plushie cries) near the toy's eyes and finish the blobs with a short line. If you pull the bottle away from the end of the tear quite quickly, it will make the line taper off nicely like a real tear shape.

Snot
Much like the splash in the vomit picture (at right), anything lime green, blob-like and near a creature's nose will read as snot. Apply 2 different shades of green for extra gross-out-ness. Essentially, making a splash is much like blood drips, except now the blobs and lines meet in the center of the splash shape rather than following a cut line. To make good snot, make more free-form splash shapes—it looks more natural.

Drool
Drool is basically one blob and a very thin line of paint back to the corner of the mouth.

Vomit
Vomit can be more difficult than other fluids. I find the look of big areas of dimensional paint unappealing, so it's more like creating a thin stream of bile. You can wiggle your line down from the mouth of your creature to indicate the journey this unpleasantness has taken. A small, tasteful splash says so much more than vomit-a-palooza. (Add bits of carrot at your discretion.)

Artist Tips

✪ Are these techniques "too much" for your toy? Where should you place the blood or other bodily fluids? To give yourself some removable embellishments, apply your paint to a very smooth plastic surface, such as an ice-cream-container lid, and peel it off when it's dry. You can then try out the shapes on your toy without permanently altering it. Move your paint around until you come up with something that looks good, then apply the actual paint to the toy in the same way.

✪ If you find this difficult to do freehand, draw your shapes on a piece of paper and practice by tracing over them.

Rabbit Girl, The Bunny and The Executive Angel

Artist Insider

Natascha Rosenberg
www.nataschasrosenberg.com • Madrid, Spain

If you won the lottery, what would you buy for your plush/crafty business?

A lot of fabrics, a new sewing machine with all kind of features and a studio with some space for silkscreening.

Forest
Treelings

onegirl designwrks

www.onegirldesignwrks.blogspot.com • Melbourne, Australia

What are your goals for your plush business?

*I'm enjoying making things just for fun at the moment.
The more oobees I can sell, the more fun I get to have making
them——so that's my motivation for the moment.*

Oobee

Bears

O Giant One,
Running Bunny
and Cranky Girl

Artist Insider

Mandy Jouan

www.sappymoosetree.com • Chula Vista, California

What's your dream job?

Ever since I was a wee girl, I've been in love with theater productions. If I could pick anything to do, I'd love to work building props like puppets or other toy-like things for movies and other productions.

Zombie Sock Monkeys

Felt Snails

We're good snails. We won't eat your plants (although you can make us some special felt lettuce when we're looking hungry). We're much better behaved than the snails living in your flowerpots.

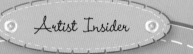

Artist Insider

Emerald Mosley

www.goldtop.org/craft • London, England

What's your favorite extracurricular activity?
Dancing with the Actionettes (www.actionettes.com).

Necessities

- felt—any color (wool if possible; it cuts cleaner and feels nicer!)
- acrylic or fabric paints
- stuffing material
- toy beads, dried beans or rice
- embroidery thread
- sewing thread
- drawing utensil
- pins
- needles
- scissors

Cut and mark pattern

1 Photocopy the pattern (on page 138) and scale to the desired size. Cut out the pieces and mark 1 side of the shell, horn and body pieces with the letter A. Mark the other side of each piece with the letter B.

Cut pieces

2 Lay all patterns on the felt, A sides up (where applicable). Trace and cut them. Repeat with the B sides up for the shell, horn and snail body pieces. (This hides any drawing when you place the pieces together.) Trace the patterns and cut out the shapes until you have a total of 2 shell pieces, 2 horn pieces, 1 body, 1 foot and 1 lettuce leaf.

Create eyes

3 Paint an eye on side A of 1 of your body pieces and on side B of the other 1. Set aside to dry completely.

Embroider shell

4 Draw a spiral on the wrong side of each of the shell pieces to act as a guide when you stitch. Decorate the shell using lines of spaced backstitch and French knots. (See "Snaily Stitches" at right.) Leave a ⅛" (3mm) seam around the edge of the shell. Also leave a ⅛" (3mm) "gutter" in a spiral shape on each piece for a defining spiral once your shell is stuffed.

Sew body, foot and tail pieces together

5 Sew the 2 halves of the body to the foot using small running stitches. Start from the tail and narrow end of the foot, working toward the head. As you run out of foot to sew, join the two halves of the body. As you are sewing the two curved edges together, the fabric should appear to buckle a bit, but, in fact, it's the 2 flat pieces of fabric becoming a third thing! Sew around the tail, stopping after about 1" (3cm).

Create shell and finish

6 Line up the shells by placing a pin through the middle of each shell. Slot the 2 halves of the shell over each side of the body, stitching them in position by continuing the running stitch through the shell, then the body, then the shell pieces. Sew around the head, making sure you sew the horns in place between the 2 pieces of body as you go. Sew to within 1" (3cm) of the end of the head, then stuff the body with toy stuffing and a few toy beads to add weight, making the snail stable enough to stand. Sew around the shell, leaving a 1" (3cm) opening. Stuff with toy stuffing. Complete sewing to close the shell. Sew a line of running stitch in a spiral to define the shape of the shell. (It might be a bit of a struggle going through the stuffing, but persevere—it looks great when it's done!)

Snaily Stitches—Use a combination of these techniques to embellish your snail shell:

❀ **Backstitch; spaced and unspaced**

Bring your needle and thread up from the back to the front of the felt. Go back about a stitch length. Go through to the back of the felt, making a stitch, and come up through the front of the felt about a stitch length for unspaced backstitch (or two for spaced back stitch). Repeat.

❀ **French knot**

Bring your needle and thread up from the back to the front of the felt. Holding the thread taught, wrap it twice or three times (this will vary the size of the knot) around the needle. Making sure you hold the thread behind the needle as you push down, stitch down through the felt near to where you came up. Make sure you don't go back through the same hole or your knot will disappear!

❀ **Ermine fill (on snail horns)**

Make a vertical straight stitch, then overlap with a cross stitch. This makes a six-pointed star.

Owls

Artist Insider

Sewing Stars
www.sewingstars.com • Providence, Rhode Island

What's your worst plushie-making experience?
*I once made a doll and decided to give her yarn hair. Even though
I was adding the yarn in pieces over only a 2"-square area, it took forever!*

50

Eye Can See You
and Señor Acorn

Artist Insider

Michelle Valigura
www.thegirlsproductions.com • South Pasadena, California

Suicide Kittens
www.suicidekittens.com • New York, New York

Artist Insider

Is this your full-time job? If not, what is?

I love plushies, but kittens do not pay the rent. In addition to Suicide Kittens, I work as a freelance designer and an administrative assistant.

Angelo
the
Kitten

Poof

Wiggles

Artist Insider

Boofyboof (Kaela)

www.boofyboof.com • Seattle, Washington

What's your inspiration?

I'm inspired by Poof Wiggles because they're inspired by boots, celery, sweaters, bug bites, funny words, green beans, ballard, paranoia, boofs, peanut butter, burrowing and the snug.

5

Candy Corn Doll

I love Halloween, plain and simple. It's one of my favorite holidays. I won't go bad or run out after Halloween, so you can enjoy my candy cuteness all year long!

Necessities

white craft felt—one 9" × 12" (23cm × 30cm) sheet

orange craft felt—two 9" × 12" (23cm × 30cm) sheets

yellow craft felt—one 9" × 12" (23cm × 30cm) sheet

stuffing material

thread to match

black craft paint

drawing utensil

paintbrush

scissors

needle or sewing machine

1 **Trace and cut pieces**
Trace pattern pieces (page 135) on felt and cut out all pieces as follows: 1 top from white felt, 1 midsection from orange felt, and 1 bottom section from yellow felt.

2 **Paint face**
Use black craft paint to paint facial features on 1 side of the orange midsection piece; let it dry for 15 to 20 minutes.

3 **Sew and press seams**
With right sides facing, sew the top and the bottom pieces to the midsection. This will make the front of the doll. Press down the seams.

4 **Attach back piece and stuff**
With right sides facing, pin together and sew the full front piece to the remaining 9" x 12" (23cm x 30cm) piece of orange craft felt. The back of the doll will be solid orange. Sew around the top and sides leaving a ⅜" (1cm) seam allowance. Leave an opening at the bottom where indicated. Trim seams and snip curves, remove the pins, turn right-side out and stuff doll. Whipstitch opening closed.

Artist Insider

Denise Cozzitorto
www.heydayfashion.com • Sacramento, California

Betty
the Yeti

Artist Insider

Serena Kuhl

www.flickr.com/photos/pocti • Northern Territory, Australia

Is this your full-time job? If not, what is?

I'm a senior high art teacher.

Black Kitty,
Pretty Pink Girl
and Orange Dog

Artist Insider

Felt Friends
www.feltfriends.com • Seattle, Washington

What tools do you use to stuff your plush?
I use a plastic palm tree for stuffing my small plushies.

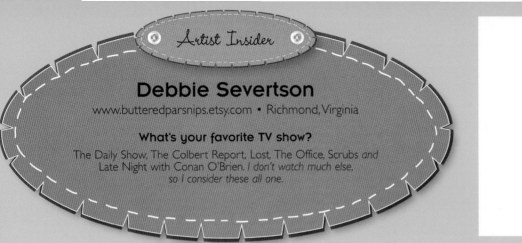

Artist Insider

Debbie Severtson

www.butteredparsnips.etsy.com • Richmond, Virginia

What's your favorite TV show?

The Daily Show, The Colbert Report, Lost, The Office, Scrubs *and*
Late Night with Conan O'Brien. *I don't watch much else,*
so I consider these all one.

Owl

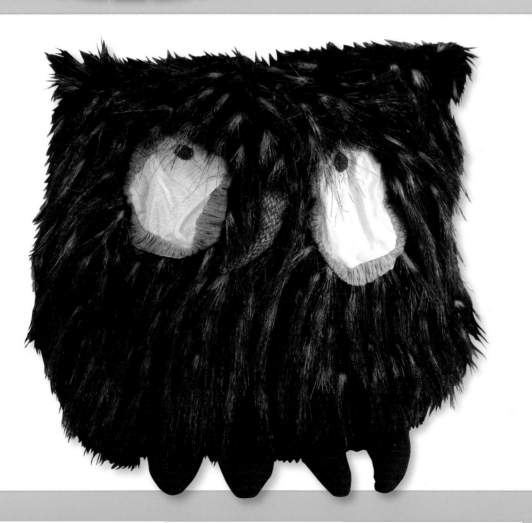

Flutter Dragon, Amelia and Ren

Artist Insider

BridgeTroll

www.bridgetroll.net • Albuquerque, New Mexico

What's your inspiration?

I like to make up stories and draw with my children. Most of the time that's where my characters come from. Sometimes I think of a word or phrase and I imagine what it would look like if it were a plush. Sometimes I think of a person and imagine what it would be like if she...

Mitsy and Bitsy

Artist Insider

Sam Lamb

www.samlamb.blogspot.com • Toronto, Canada

What's your favorite fabric?

*This is too easy; I think I was born to love wool. Patterns on fabric are gre[...]
but it's the feel of wool that really gets me going. Blankets, suiting,
balls of merino, cashmere…there's just so much wool to love.
Natural fibers rock, hands down.*

5

Plushood (Shlomi Schillinger and Tamar Moshkovitz)

www.plushood.com • Tel Aviv, Israel

What's your best plushie-making experience?

Seeing our first Pinto alive after a long time of planning.

Plushoods:
Pinto, Miss Moss
and Jose

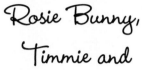

Rosie Bunny, Timmie and Roma Ritz

Artist Insider

Marilyn Patrizio

www.mpatrizio.blogspot.com • Brooklyn, New York

What's your inspiration?

I am greatly inspired by the character designs I see in street art, Japanese "kawaii" culture and the concept of making something extraordinary out of simple objects and tools.

Wiggle, the Sweater-Wearing Tooth

Wiggle lives in your head. No, he's not a figment of your imagination—in fact, he's more real than you'd like. Wiggle sits next to your sweet tooth, gathering wooly sweaters to make your usually fresh mouth feel as if you've been chewing on dirt and cotton balls. His only mortal enemy is a toothbrush with a big dollop of your favorite toothpaste. You'll have to decide for yourself if you want him to move out or if you just want to strip him of his sweaters.

Necessities

- off-white fabric
- old sweater
- white felt
- black felt
- stuffing material
- thread
- colored pencil or tailor's chalk
- turning tool
- pins
- needles
- scissors
- rotary cutter and mat (optional)
- sewing machine (optional)

Artist Insider

David Huyck
www.bunchofmonkeys.com • Carrboro, North Carolina

1. Cut pieces

Using the pattern pieces (on page 135), cut 1 crown, 1 root, and 2 body pieces from your off-white fabric. Leave a consistent seam allowance of between ⅛" (3mm) and ¼" (6mm).

2. Cut sweater pieces

Cut 2 strips out of the old sweater to about 2½" x 7½" (6cm x 19cm), long enough to cover the tooth's body pattern. Don't leave a seam allowance for these pieces.

3. Create eye

Cut a semi-circle from the white felt and a wedge from the black felt for the eye. Again, no need to leave a seam allowance, though the bottom edges of the eye pieces will be covered by the sweater.

4. Appliqué eyes and sweater

Draw a line across the tooth body pieces on the right side where you'll place the top edge of the sweater strips—make sure the line is in the same place for both pieces. Appliqué the white eye piece first, slightly overlapping the line you placed in the last step. Add the black eye piece in the same way. Appliqué the sweater strips onto the body of the tooth using a zigzag stitch on your machine, or a whipstitch if you are working by hand. See the "Artist Tip" (at right) for a tip to keep the raveling tendencies of the sweater under control.

5. Attach crown and roots to body

Align one half of the crown piece with one of the body pieces, facing the sweater side to the crown piece you're attaching, and sew together. The curves at the edges can be tricky to pin, so take your time. Fold the sewn section out of the way and align the other body piece with the other half of the crown, again facing the sweater side to the crown piece. Sew to attach. Repeat for roots. All the pieces except for the arms should be together now, with only the sides left open.

6. Create tooth surface

With the tooth still wrong-side out, pull out the fabric of the crown piece and crease it down the middle. Sew a curved line from about ¼ of the width to about ¾ of the width of the whole crown piece. In the middle of the trapped fabric, snip out a small wedge. At the snip you just made, 90-degrees to the first crease, fold the crown again. Sew another curve in the middle ⅓ of the width of the whole crown piece.

7. Turn and stuff

Turn the tooth right-side out through 1 of the open sides, poking out the roots and curves with your turning tool (unsharpened pencil, chopstick, etc.). Stuff the tooth, using small wads to jam into the narrower sections and progressing to larger wads as you fill it up.

8. Create useless arms

Cut 2 small rectangles about 2½" x 4" (6cm x 10cm) from the sweater material for the arms. Fold the rectangles lengthwise and sew one short end and the long open side using the zigzag stitch on your machine or a whipstitch if sewing by hand. Turn the arms right-side out and put a small amount of stuffing inside. Don't fill them completely—leave the open ends flat so you can sew through them easily. Pin the arms into the open sides of the tooth, placing the open ends inside the unsewn openings. With your thread and needle, sew up the sides using a whipstitch, making sure to secure the arms in place. (Just before closing the tooth completely, adjust the amount of stuffing to your desired firmness).

Artist Tip

If your chosen sweater is 100 percent wool (some say anything over 50 percent will work), you can felt the sweater first by running it through the agitation cycle of your washing machine with a little bit of soap in hot water. This will help prevent unraveling. It may take a few cycles to get the sweater to felt as much as you'd like. Note: This will shrink your sweater, so don't over-felt to the point that there isn't enough sweater to fit on the tooth.

Horse,
Bunny and
Bear

Artist Insider

Samantha Salway

www.plump-pudding.co.uk • Wenvoe Vale of Glamorgan, United Kingdom

Where's the best place you get fabric?

Anywhere and everywhere: Internet, car-boots sale, thrift shops and retail.

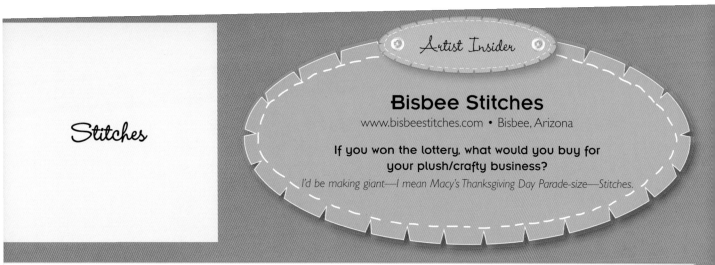

Stitches

Bisbee Stitches

www.bisbeestitches.com • Bisbee, Arizona

If you won the lottery, what would you buy for your plush/crafty business?

I'd be making giant—I mean Macy's Thanksgiving Day Parade-size—Stitches.

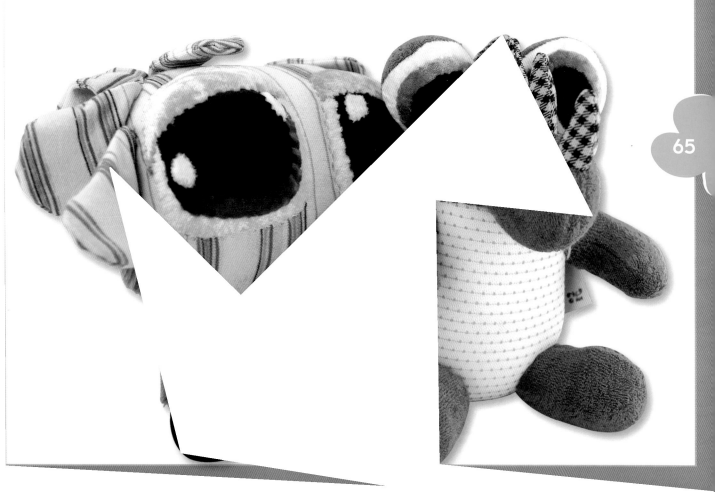

65

Lustful Luanne,
Henry Envy
and Greedy Helene

Artist Insider

Fawne DeRosia

www.momentofstars.com • Thomaston, Georgia

Do you have your own collection of toys and/or plush?

Yes, and my little girl plays with my collection more than I do.

Karin Yamagiwa Madan

Redmond, Washington

Why do you do this?

*Much of my artistic inspiration comes from my mom.
I doubt I'd be doing this had it not been for her.*

Sorry and
Lone Cone
Without a Home

Sasha the Whale Pin (and Friends)

I love to see the world. Green tends to be my favorite color, but I also really like blue. I enjoy the outdoors.

Necessities

- two colors of felt (wool or acrylic)
- options for embellishing: beads, sequins, felt shapes or colorful thread
- embroidery floss
- stuffing material
- thread
- glue gun
- pin back or magnet
- embroidery needle
- needle
- scissors

Artist Insider

Kristen Rask

www.schmancytoys.com • Seattle, Washington

What's your next vacation destination?

Not sure. Do I have time for a vacation?

Cut pieces

1 Use the pattern (on page 134) to cut out 2 felt pieces for the whale body. You can shrink or enlarge the pattern to the size desired. Cut out 1 piece of water spray from your felt. Choose a color that is complementary to the whale's body.

Add embellishments

2 Embellish 1 piece of the whale body and/or water spray however you like. Some fun examples include a French knot or colonial knot for the eye or as a decoration; beads or buttons for eyes; backstitch or outline stitch for a mouth; a running stitch along the water spray; a small felt heart or other simple shape to be glued to the body; embroidery on a fin; or embroidery on the body with fun stitches such as the eyelet stitch, star stitch or seed stitch.

Sew pieces together

3 Now that your whale's looking pretty, put it together. I hand sew my whales. Starting at the tail, use a blanket stitch all the way around the outside of the body. Make sure to leave a ½" (1cm) to 1" (3cm) opening for stuffing.

Stuff and close

4 Use the batting to stuff your whale. It helps to find a small device to stuff the tail. I use a spear from a small vinyl toy I have at home. Once the whale is stuffed to the desired plumpness, stitch the rest of the body closed.

Use glue gun to finish

5 Use your glue gun to attach the water spray to the back of the whale. Also using your glue gun, attach a pin backing or magnet to the back of the body. If you prefer, you could sew on the pin back.

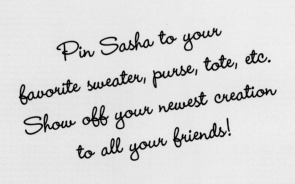

Pin Sasha to your favorite sweater, purse, tote, etc. Show off your newest creation to all your friends!

Artist Tip

If you choose to embellish your water spray, I recommend cutting out two identical pieces. Once you've embellished one piece, glue the other to its back. This hides your stitching.

Meryll (penguin),
Friedrich (robot)
and
Sosa

Artist Insider

Wendy Crabb
www.greengirlart.com • Long Island City, New York

What's your best plushie-making experience?
The best experience comes after, when the customer reacts
to the plush. It's so enjoyable to watch them squeeze.

Poppe Vera, Poppe Fleur and Poppe Olivia

Artist Insider

Berber Vos
www.kisskus.nl • Baarn, Netherlands

What's your favorite tool?
Seam rippers are essential for anyone who sews.

71

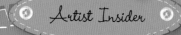

Artist Insider

Heidi Kenney

www.mypapercrane.com • Waynesboro, Pennsylvania

What do you listen to while you work on plush?

Sometimes podcasts—I love the crafty interview ones.

Ice Cream and
Ice Cream
Sandwiches

Artist Insider

Ivy Russell

www.pinned.blah.net • San Diego, California

What's your inspiration?

Buttons are a huge inspiration. I have a fairly large collection of them and will frequently go into an antiques store looking for that jar of buttons I know they have. They're shiny, inexpensive, easy to store, and it's so hard to find a button that is truly ugly or useless.

Lindy, Opal and Drew

Piggy Pouch

I'm here to celebrate the Chinese Year of the Pig. But you can use me as a piggy bank. Unfortunately, my eye was poked out because I tried to stop a much-needed shopping spree. Not that negative shopping advice justifies poking an eye out, but no one should come between a gal and a new pair of shoes!

Necessities

- 8½" x 11" (22cm x 28cm) pouch fabric
- 8½" x 11" (22cm x 28cm) liner fabric
- 8½" x 11" (22cm x 28cm) fusible lightweight interfacing
- 7" x 7" (18cm x 18cm) contrasting fabric for ears
- 2" x 2" (5cm x 5cm) square of black felt for eye
- 2½" x 2½" (6cm x 6cm) fabric for heart eye patch
- 7" (18cm) of ½" (1cm) lace ribbon
- 7" (18cm) of ½" (1cm) satin ribbon
- thread to match pouch color
- black embroidery floss
- Fray Check
- one magnetic snap
- drawing utensil
- pins
- small hand-needle (#11)
- large embroidery needle
- fabric scissors
- paper scissors
- sewing machine
- carbon paper (optional)

Artist Insider

tsai-fi

www.tsai-fi.com • Los Angeles, California

Who is your favorite plush artist?

Uglydoll. They started it all!

1. Trace and cut pieces

Photocopy the patterns (on page 139) and cut out all the paper pieces A through G. Next, lay pieces on the correct fabric and cut as follows: A (pouch side)—1 from pouch fabric, 1 from lining, 1 from interfacing; B (pouch side)—4; C (eye)—1; D (eye patch)—1 (use Fray Check to seal the edges if the fabric's edge can unravel; let it dry); E (lining)—2 from lining, 2 from interfacing; F (front and back pouch)—2 from pouch fabric; G (snout)—1. (The dotted lines on the patterns indicate a seam allowance.)

2. Sew ribbon and lace together

Pin the lace ribbon on top of the satin ribbon, then sew together.

3. Mark placement for ears, eyes, snout and eye patch

Use a needle and thread to hand mark where the ears, eyes, snout and eye patch will go by placing F on top of the front of the pouch piece. If you have access to carbon paper, place the carbon paper facedown on the fabric, place piece F on top of the fabric and trace the eye, eye patch and snout so they show up on the fabric.

4. Pin and sew eye, eye patch and snout

Pin C (eye) right-side up on F, matching the location from the previous step. Sew the eye with your sewing machine. Then pin G (snout) to F, making sure to match the location and sew it.

5. Place ribbon

Place the ribbon right-side up on F from the upper left to the lower right through the eye-patch location. Pin D (eye patch) right-side up on top of F so the ribbon is sandwiched between the 2 pieces of fabric, and sew down.

6. Create nostrils

Using embroidery floss and a hand needle, sew 2 big stitches for nostrils on G using the guidelines you marked in Step 3.

7. Create and attach ears

Pin right sides of B (ears) together. Sew from dot to dot, making sure to leave the area marked "opening" unsewn. Turn the ears right-side out through the opening. Make sure to sew both of the ears. Pin the opening of the ears matching the marked ear location on F and sew in place.

8. Complete outside of pouch

Next, pin A to F with the face on it, making sure to line up the triangles. The ends of A will roughly match to the innermost points of the ears on F front with face. Next, sew them down. Pin the blank F to the unsewn side of A and sew right sides together. Make sure to clip V-shaped curves in the seam allowance. The outside of the pouch is complete.

9. Sew lining

Fuse the interfacing to the wrong side of lining pieces E and A. Next, pin A to E, matching the triangles to each other. Sew all the way around. Pin the other E to the unsewn side of A, matching triangles and placing right sides together. When you sew the pieces together, leave the marked areas from A to B open. The lining is complete.

10. Attach snaps and liner

Using the snap placement marks on F from Step 3, align the magnetic snaps and affix to the right sides of the fabric. Pin the liner and the outer-pouch right sides together and sew along the top of the pouch. Pull the entire pouch inside out through the opening in the lining area from Step 9. Take a hand needle and some thread and sew the opening that you pulled the pouch through by making a stitch on one side of the opening and going through the opposite side. Repeat until opening is completely closed.

Now you have a piggy pouch that's ready to be filled with lots of moola!

Free-floo

Artist Insider

Jenny Harada
www.jennyharada.com • Pickerington, Ohio

What's your favorite sewing machine?
My Husqvarna 750. I like it even better than my new car.

Boot and Sissi

Artist Insider

Arbito

www.arbito.com • Seattle, Washington

Do you have your own collection of toys and/or plush?
I have a large collection of Soul of Chogokin bots.

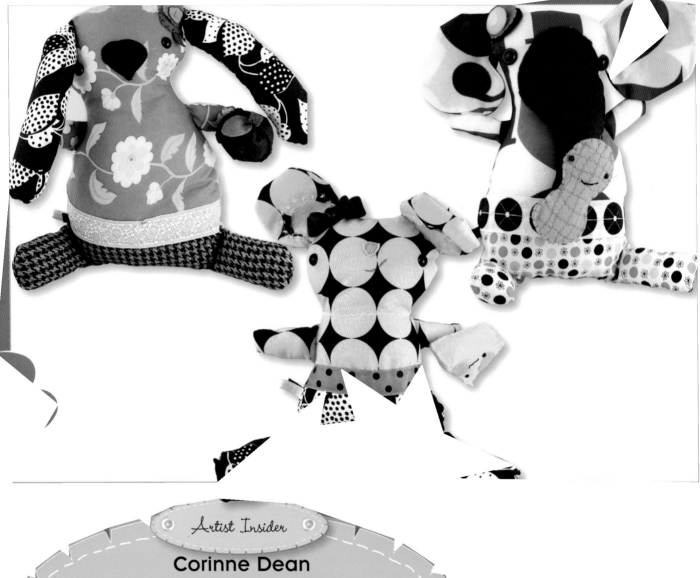

Artist Insider

Corinne Dean

www.nottoopink.etsy.com • Covington, Kentucky

Why do you do this?

I make this stuff because it makes me so darn happy—and it's a great excuse to keep buying fabric! I have a daughter and about fifteen nieces and nephews constantly inspiring me with ideas. I have to make these weird little things to clear my head…and make way for the many other strange things to pop in!

Plumpkin Robots

Artist Insider

Chrystal Myers

www.plumpkin.ca • British Columbia, Canada

What's your favorite fabric?

*I just adore Kaffe Fassett fabrics, but he is in a dead heat with Denise Schmidt.
I love their bold color choices.*

Love Bot

Artist Insider

Chad Jacobsen
Seattle, Washington

What's your dream job?
If someone would pay me to hang out at my house and play ukulele with my friends, that would be awesome.

Artist Insider

Anna Chambers
Burbank, California

What's your favorite sandwich?
Well, the sandwich is one of my favorite foods. I like all kinds, especially with avocado and a great bread.

Leaf Trio

Little Owl and Her Mommy

Who, who am I always with? My mommy, that's who, who. She brings me good things to eat and says one day I'll be able to fly from the nest. I don't know if that's wise, though; the ground looks very hard and very far down.

Necessities

small amounts of worsted-weight yarn in brown, yellow, tan and orange

9mm plastic eyes with safety backings

stuffing material

thread

crochet hook size G/6 (4mm)

darning needle

sewing needle

Artist Insider

Ana Paula Rimoli

www.anapaulaoli.etsy.com • Philadelphia, Pennsylvania

What's your inspiration?

My two girls, Oli and Martina, the toys I loved (and still do) when I was little, and the arts and crafts from Uruguay that have a warm, down-to-earth feeling that I really like.

Crochet Abbreviations

ch = chain

dc = double crochet

hdc = half double crochet (UK: htr, half-treble crochet)

dec = decrease

R = round

sc = single crochet (UK: dc double crochet)

sk = skip

sl st = slip st (UK: sc single crochet)

st(s) = stitch(es)

* = repeat directions between * and * as many times as indicated

Mommy Owl

Make 2 eye "roundies"
Use the yellow yarn.
R1: Ch 3, 6 hdc in the third chain from the hook
R2: 2 hdc in each hdc around (12 sts)
R3: *Sc 1, 2 sc in next hdc*, repeat 6 times (18 sts)
Bind off, leaving the long tail for sewing; set aside.

Create body
Start with the brown yarn.
R1: Ch 2, 6 sc in the second chain from the hook
R2: 2 sc in each sc around (12 sts)
R3: *Sc 1, 2 sc in next sc*, repeat 6 times (18 sts)
R4: *Sc 2, 2 sc in next sc*, repeat 6 times (24 sts)
R5: *Sc 3, 2 sc in next sc*, repeat 6 times (30 sts)
R6: *Sc 4, 2 sc in next sc*, repeat 6 times (36 sts)
R7–12: Sc 36
Change to the tan yarn.
R13–18: Sc 36
R19: *Sc 5, 2 sc in next sc*, repeat 6 times (42 sts)
R20-28: Sc 42
R29: *Sc 5, dec 1*, repeat 6 times (36 sts)
R30: *Sc 4, dec 1*, repeat 6 times (30 sts)
R31: *Sc 3, dec 1*, repeat 6 times (24 sts)

Assemble face
Sew the eye "roundies" in place, attach the plastic eyes,
embroider the beak with the orange yarn.
R32: *Sc 2, dec 1*, repeat 6 times (18 sts)
R33: *Sc 1, dec 1*, repeat 6 times (12 sts)

Finish body
Stuff the body.
R34: *Sk 1 sc, sc 1*, repeat 6 times (6 sts)
Sl st in the next st, bind off, weave in the loose ends.

Crochet and attach wings
R1: Ch 2, 6 sc in the second chain from the hook
R2: 2 sc in each sc around (12 sts)
R3-10: Sc 12
Sl st in the next st, bind off, leaving the long tail for sewing,
sew the open end together, sew to the body (no need to
stuff them).

Baby Owl

Make 2 eye "roundies"
Use the yellow yarn.
R1: Ch 3, 6 hdc in the third chain from the hook
R2: 2 sc in each hdc around (12 sts)
Bind off, leaving the long tail for sewing; set aside.

Create body
Start with the brown yarn.
R1: Ch 2, 6 sc in the second chain from the hook
R2: 2 sc in each sc around (12 sts)
R3: *Sc 1, 2 sc in next sc*, repeat 6 times (18 sts)
R4: *Sc 2, 2 sc in next sc*, repeat 6 times (24 sts)
R5-8: Sc 24
Change to the tan yarn.
R9–14: Sc 24

Assemble face
Sew the eye "roundies" in place; attach the plastic eyes,
embroider the beak with the orange yarn.
R15: *Sc 3, 2 sc in the next sc*, repeat 6 times (30 sts)
R16–18: Sc 30
R19: *Sc 3, dec 1*, repeat 6 times (24 sts)
R20: *Sc 2, dec 1*, repeat 6 times (18 sts)
R21: *Sc 1, dec 1*, repeat 6 times (12 sts)

Finish body
Stuff teh body.
R22: *Sk 1 sc, sc 1*, repeat 6 times (6 sts)
Sl st in the next st, bind off, weave in the loose end.

Crochet and attach wings
R1: Ch 2, 5 sc in the second chain from the hook
R2: 2 sc in each sc around (10 sts)
R3–7: Sc 10
Sl st in the next st, bind off, leaving the long tail for sewing
(no need to stuff them); sew the open end together, sew to
the body.

Listo!

Artist Insider

Courtney Barnebey
Seattle, Washington

What's your favorite fabric?
Unbleached muslin—I love the look.

Softbot

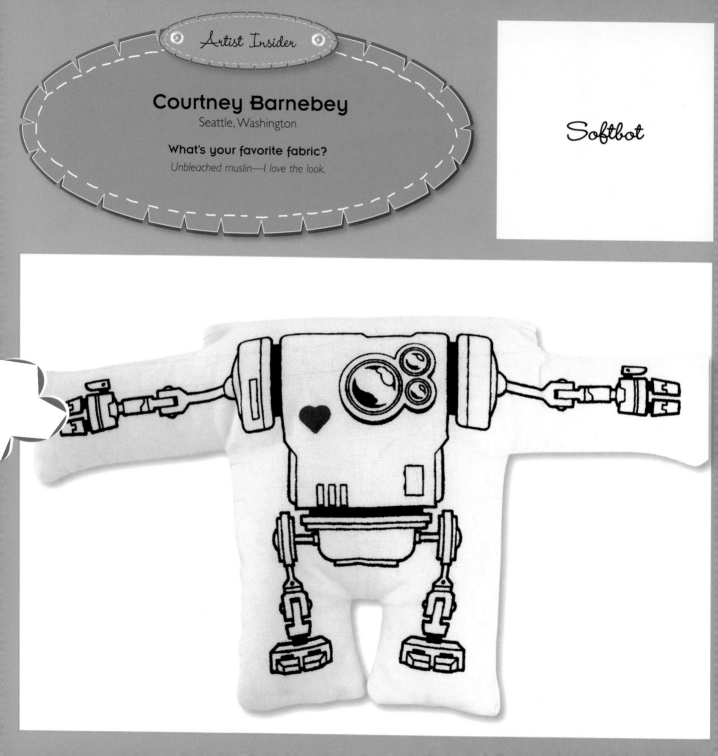

Family of Whales:
Daddy Gray,
Mooma Blue and
Baby Cornflower

Artist Insider

Blair Stocker

www.blairpeter.typepad.com • Seattle, Washington

Do you have a helpful hint?

*Never leave home without a cute tote bag to lug around
all your crafting supplies.*

Mr. Kitty,
Red Devil Baby
and Mr. Kitty

Artist Insider

Max Badger
www.maxbadger.com • Seattle, Washington

Do you have your own collection of toys and/or plush?

Yes! I love Qees; I have about thirty. Older He-Man action figures and Star Wars toys, too.

Melancholia

Artist Insider

Ryan Myers
Long Island, New York

What's your favorite extracurricular activity?
Painting or maybe watching my newborn son sleep.

Cockeyed Sock Monkeys

We come in all different shapes and sizes. In fact, now that we think about it, not one of us is the same…the only thing we have in common is our stuffing. We love to sit around the house—on beds, or shelves…couches are nice, too. You'd be surprised at how flexible we are; you can tie us in a pretzel, or around your neck—whatever you please. Oh, and because we're cockeyed, it just so happens we have 40/40 vision (okay, only in one eye)…so of course, we always keep an eye on you to make sure you keep your mischievousness to a minimum.

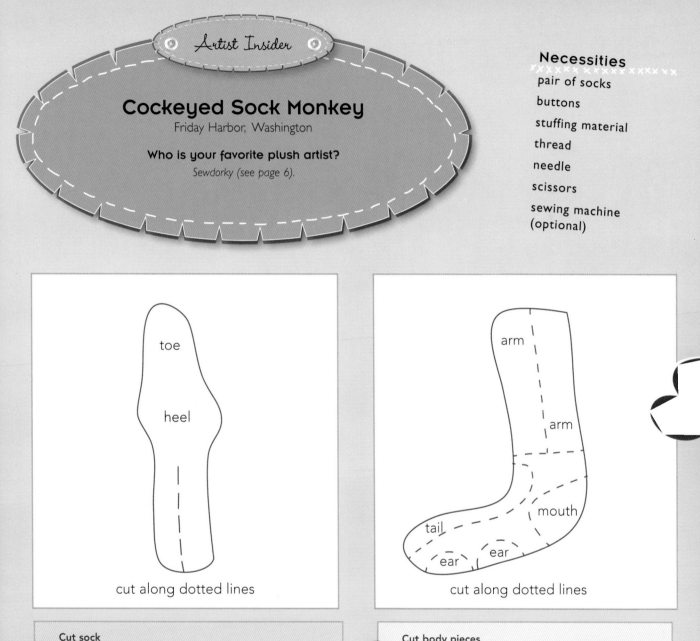

Cockeyed Sock Monkey

Friday Harbor, Washington

Who is your favorite plush artist?

Sewdorky (see page 6).

Necessities

pair of socks

buttons

stuffing material

thread

needle

scissors

sewing machine (optional)

---

toe

heel

cut along dotted lines

---

arm

arm

mouth

tail

ear   ear

cut along dotted lines

Cut sock

For the body of your sock monkey, take one sock and cut from the opening of the sock down the center. Stop cutting 1" (3cm) from the center of the heel. Turn the sock wrong-side out.

1

Cut body pieces

With the other sock, cut out the pieces for the mouth, ears, arms and tail of your sock monkey.

2

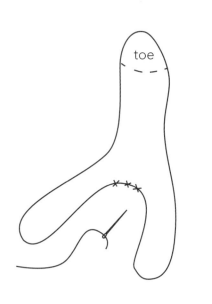

3

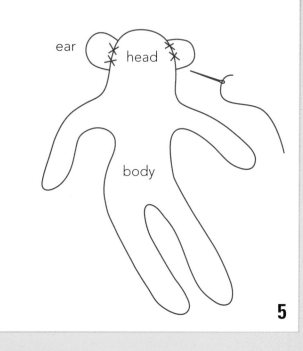

5

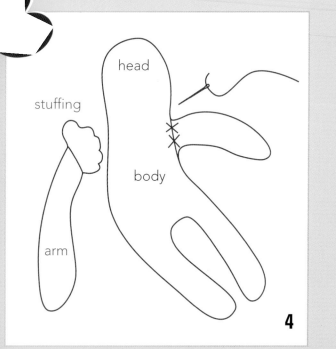

4

Create legs

3 Start sewing at the bottom of the leg, where the monkey's feet will be. Repeat with the other leg. Leave a 2" (5cm) opening for stuffing at the "crotch" of the monkey. Turn the sock right-side out and stuff your monkey. Then hand stitch the opening closed (See figure 3).

Sew and attach arms

4 Turn the arm pieces wrong-side out and sew up the middle as you did the leg pieces. Turn them right-side out and stuff them. Fold in the top of the arms slightly to hide any frayed edges, and sew the arms to the body of the monkey.

Sew and attach ears

5 Turn the ear pieces wrong-side out, then sew them together in pairs to form 2 ears. Leave a portion unsewn if you want to stuff the ears. Turn right-side out and hand stitch the ears to the sides of the head.

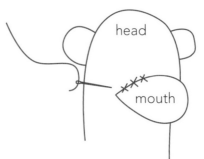

6

Sew and attach tail

Turn the tail piece wrong-side out and sew it as you did the arms and legs. Turn it right-side out and stuff it. Turn the top of the tail in slightly to hide the frayed edges as you did with the arms, and stitch it onto the heel of the body sock (the monkey's bottom).

6

Sew and attach mouth and finish

Turn the frayed edges of the cut mouth pieces inward and sew to the body of your monkey where a mouth should go. Start sewing at the top of the mouth and stitch. When you get to the corners, fold inward to make a 30- to 40-degree angle, so that corners of the mouth come to a point. When you have about 1" (3cm) left to sew around the mouth, stuff the mouth, then finish sewing the mouth to the monkey's head. Sew buttons on the face for eyes and sew the remaining thread on top of the monkey's head for hair.

7

7

Artist Insider

Lauren Faust

www.milkywayandthegalaxygirls.com • Los Angeles, California

Is this your full-time job? If not, what is?

I work in the animation industry as a writer/producer/story artist for the Cartoon Network show Foster's Home for Imaginary Friends.

Pluto,
Galaxy Girl

tsai-fi

www.tsai-fi.com • Los Angeles, California

What's your favorite tool?

I use E6000 glue in my craft studio.

So Strawberry, Nerdy Birdy and Cherry Marine

Love=Creature:
Odwaga the Piggy,
Babka Genowefa
and Krolik,
and Uggla the Owl

Artist Insider

Dawn Ramerman

www.lookwhaticando.etsy.com • Seattle, Washington

What do you listen to while you work on plush?

*I watch TV while I make plush. I get to create and watch Project Runway,
Cash Cab, America's Next Top Model or something on HGTV.
It's a super excuse to get some TV time.*

Oneye: She-Devil

and

Oneye: Cats

★ Artist Insider ★

12Punt3
www.12punt3.nl/shop.html • The Hague, Netherlands

What's the weirdest tool you use to create your plushies?

A plastic No. 9 knitting needle. I use it to stuff my Oneyes. That way I can make sure that all the filling is divided all over. I use quite a bit of force to get it stuffed the way I want, so the needle keeps breaking. I started with a long needle and now I have only one-fourth of it left!

Sprout King
and
Sprout Babies

Pale
and
Lime

Camilla Engman
www.camillaengman.com • Gothenburg, Sweden

Darling Bacon

I'm Darling Bacon. I'm fun to be around, whether you like your friends to have a soft side or be a little crispy.

Dearie Toast

I'm Dearie Toast. I came from a truckstop diner, so I have a harder edge and sometimes I curse—but I don't know better. I have a very good heart, even though I'm sometimes called a rebel.

Dishy Egg

I'm Dishy Egg. I'm a free spirit and a joy to be around. My best friend is Dearie Toast. I like picnics, backgammon and strawberries.

Artist Insider

Mucho

www.schmancy.etsy.com • Seattle, Washington

What do you listen to while you work on plush?

Whatever John Waters suggests.

Necessities

felt—light brown and dark brown for toast, yellow and white for egg, red and white for bacon

stuffing material

embroidery thread—dark brown for toast, white for egg, red for bacon

fabric glue

glue gun or all-purpose, permanent adhesive

embroidery needle

Dearie Toast Magnet

1 **Cut pieces**
Using the pattern pieces (on page 135), trace and cut 1 of Figure 1 and 1 of Figure 2 from the light brown felt. Trace and cut 1 of Figure 1 from the dark brown felt.

2 **Embroider face**
Embroider a face on Fig. 2. I used a French knot for the eyes and a straight stitch for the smile, but feel free to do it any way you like.

3 **Glue and sew figures together**
Glue Fig. 2 in the center of the darker Fig. 1 using fabric glue. Allow the glue to dry. Stitch the Fig. 1 pieces together and stuff before finishing.

4 **Attach magnet**
Using a glue gun or an all-purpose, permanent adhesive, glue the magnet to the back of the toast.

Dishy Egg Magnet

1 **Cut pieces**
Using the pattern pieces (on page 135), trace and cut 2 Fig. 1 shapes from the white felt. Using the pattern pieces, trace and cut 1 of the Fig. 2 shape from the yellow felt.

2 **Embroider face**
Embroider a face on Fig. 2 as you wish. I used a French knot for the eyes and a straight stitch for the smile.

3 **Glue and sew figures together**
Glue Fig. 2 to the top of 1 of the Fig. 1 pieces using fabric glue. Allow the glue to dry. Stitch the Fig. 1 pieces together and stuff the egg before stitching it closed.

4 **Attach magnet**
Using a glue gun or an all-purpose, permanent adhesive, glue the magnet to back of the egg.

Darling Bacon Magnet

1 **Cut bacon pieces**
Cut 2 pieces of red felt in a wavy shape for bacon. Cut 2 slim strips from white felt.

2 **Glue strips together**
Glue the white strips to the top of one of the red pieces and allow the glue to dry.

3 **Stitch pieces together and attach magnet**
Stitch the red pieces together, leaving a small opening to stuff. Stuff and stitch the opening closed. Using a glue gun or an all-purpose, permanent adhesive, glue the magnet to the back of the bacon.

(⊙) Artist Insider (⊙)

Andrea Stern

www.stitchinkitten.com • Chauncey, Ohio

Do your prefer cake or pie?

*A few years ago I taught at ArtFest and saw Teesha Moore's wonderful
Pink and Orange journal and was inspired to come home and make
my birthday cake of neon-orange cake with shocking pink frosting.*

Plurtle

and

Swanson Swims

Birds on a Wire

Artist Insider

Amanda Etches-Johnson
www.etches-johnson.com • Toronto, Ontario

Where do you sell stuff?
I hardly sell my stuff anymore, but when I do it's at a couple of local shops in the Toronto area and on my Web site.

Cutesypoo

www.cutesypoo.blogspot.com • Burnaby, British Columbia

What's the weirdest tool you use to create your plushies?

I don't know why, but I use the sharp end of my scissors to stuff my toys. It works better than the end of a chopstick as long as you're careful to stuff first with just your fingers then use the scissors to really stuff it in just right.

Lilac Pup Pup,
Strawberry Skunk
and Tabby Kitty

Bashful Boris and Little Blind Bird, and Louie-Marcel and His Lonely Whale

Artist Insider

House of Ingri

www.houseofingri.com • Brooklyn, New York

Do you have a helpful hint?

I always have chalk on hand to mark fabric. It works on a lot of different surfaces and is easy to erase.

Blind Patagonian Penguin

I'm a native of South America, born and raised in Ituzaingo, Argentina. After wandering through Buenos Aires and hanging out with the ladies (it's said I'm made from an old skirt) for years and years, I recently migrated to North America. Here, I took a road trip from California through the Oregon Coast to Seattle. I like to be close to the water where I enjoy sunsets and long wobbly walks on the beach.

necessities

¼ yard (23cm) fabric of your choice for the penguin's body

small scrap of white fabric for the belly

black felt for the feet

strong cardboard or other material that won't bend easily for the feet

softer cardboard, folded in half, for the beak

stuffing material

matching thread

pins

scissors

sewing needle or sewing machine

iron-on interfacing for stretchy fabrics (optional)

eye materials: buttons, felt, sequins, etc. (optional)

Artist Insider

Lizette Greco
www.lizettegreco.com • Pasadena, California

Trace and cut pattern

Trace and cut the pattern pieces (on page 136) from the fabric: 1 of the body, 2 of the sides, 4 of the wings, 2 of the head, 1 of the bottom, 2 of the beak leaving an 1/8" (3mm) seam allowance. To keep stretchy fabric from changing its shape after you cut it, use iron-on interfacing. Follow the manufacturer's instructions to apply the interfacing to the back side of the cut pieces.

Trace and cut cardboard

Trace and cut the pattern pieces (on page 136) from cardboard for 2 of the feet and 1 beak. Set aside.

Attach belly piece

Trace the belly pattern (on page 136) onto the white fabric and cut. Pin the belly piece to the front of the body and hand or machine sew it in place. Pin each of the side pieces to each side of the main body piece right sides together and sew. Have the side pieces extend past the bottom of the body to have the material to form the tail. Keep the side pieces folded in over the front of the body and facing wrong-side out. Sew the side pieces together starting at the top and ending where the pieces extended past the body to form the tail. Set aside.

Create head

Pin the 2 sides of the head together, and sew leaving the bottom straight edge open. Turn the head right-side out and stuff. Note: If you want to add eyes to the penguin, you can use buttons, circles of felt or sequins. It's often easier to attach the eyes before you stuff the head. Set the head aside. Sew the beak pieces together, leaving an opening, and turn it right-side out. Insert the folded cardboard piece into the beak. Sew the beak opening closed, pin it to the head and hand stitch it into place.

Turn and stuff body

Pin the bottom piece to the base of the body and the sides and sew, leaving an opening for stuffing. Turn the penguin right-side out and stuff it, making sure you fill every edge and corner of the tail first. Also, make sure the base of the penguin sits flat, as it will keep the penguin standing after the feet are attached. After you're finished stuffing the base, sew the opening closed. Take the stuffed head, pin it in place and hand sew it to the body of the penguin. Set aside.

Create feet

Using the pattern (on page 136), trace and cut 4 of the feet from the black felt. Insert the cardboard feet between the top and bottom pieces of each foot, then sew together. When the feet are done, pin under the penguin with the "toes" sticking out from under the belly. Make sure the feet are in the right place to help the penguin stand alone before you stitch them in place.

Add wings

Pin the wings with the right sides together and sew, leaving an opening on the bottom straight edge. Turn the wings inside out and hand stitch the wings in place on each side of the penguin's body.

Artist Tips

❋ I used all recycled materials for the penguin, including the wrong side of an old skirt for the main fabric, because I liked the texture and color of it better than the "right" side of the skirt.

❋ If you want to spend more time on the feet, wings and beak, take the extra steps that I did: Cut one set of the pattern pieces for the feet, beak and wings in black felt and another set of each in black satin (with a seam allowance). Wrap the satin pieces around the cardboard and tape them into place. Hand-sew the felt to the satin side with the cardboard in between—without going through the cardboard with the needle. This step isn't necessary, but it adds a nice touch.

Quirquincho's Eye

I'm Quirquincho the armadillo. I don't see very well now, but maybe I will after you make an eye for me. My upholstery shell is durable yet huggable. I make for a handy companion and will take care of your ant problem. When I'm not slurping up insects, I like to cuddle up and read a good book.

Necessities

pencil

scissors

pins

tissue paper

embroidery needle

embroidery thread

1 Trace and cut pieces
Trace the pattern of your plushie's head and the eye onto tissue paper. Cut and pin the tissue paper onto the plushie's head, making sure the eye is in the right place.

2 Start stitching eye
Insert the needle with a single strand of thread and a knot at the edge of the eye. Stitch around until you complete the circle. Gently tear and remove the tissue paper.

3 Add more thread
Keep stitching around and inside the circle until it's filled. Make a simple knot in the middle. Insert your needle in the middle and bring it out, away from the eye. Cut the thread close to the fabric of the head. Repeat Steps 1–3 with the other eye. You can also switch colors to make pupils, or you can embroider a pupil inside a white piece of felt.

Artist Tip
 I do most of my embroidery on top of tissue paper. I trace the drawing to be embroidered on a piece of tissue paper, pin it to my fabric, embroider, then gently tear the paper away when I'm done.

Dreaming
Phoneheads

Artist Insider

Pied Nu
www.lepiednu.com • Seattle, Washington

What's your inspiration?
...dog, Roxy. She has so many facial expressions.

Artist Insider

Aimee Ray

www.dreamfollow.com • Siloam Springs, Arkansas

Do you have your own collection of toys and/or plush?

Yes! I collect toys from the 1980s (My Little Pony, Charmkins, Rose Petal, etc.) and anything else that catches my eye. My studio is full of toys.

Fey Fat Kitty, Egbert Owl and Kimiko Fat Kitty

Bunny and Cat

Friends of Little Roy: Adding Wires to Plush

I'm Little Roy, a magical corduroy doll, and these three are some of my friends. Anyone who wears corduroy can be our friend, or just say, "I'm a friend of Little Roy, too!"

Necessities
xxxxxx xxxxxx xxxxx xx

telephone wire

baling wire (very cheap, found at most hardware stores)

needle-nose pliers

fabric glue or hot glue

scissors or awl

Cut wire for embellishments

1 Do you want the wire to be bendable or really stiff? Colored telephone wire is a great flexible wire that's easily cut with scissors. Baling wire (the wire used for wrapping hay) is very stiff, and you'll need to use pliers or wire cutters to cut it. I prefer needle-nose pliers because they cut and easily bend the wires. Decide which wires you'd like to insert and where, and cut them to the appropriate lengths.

Add wires to plush

2 Add wire before or after all parts are sewn together and before stuffing by pushing the wires through the fabric from the inside. You might need to use an awl or scissors to poke holes in the fabric first. Bend the wires in half and push through two holes for a pair of legs or for a whisker on each side of a nose. Use more bent wires for more whiskers, legs or hairs. (If you want only one piece of wire to stick out of the fabric, create a knot or spiral with the other end of the wire.)

Cover holes

3 Once all the wires are added, still working from the inside of the plush, glue a small piece of fabric over each bent piece of wire with hot glue or fabric glue to keep the wire from pulling through.

Finish plushie

4 Bend wires into the desired position, then add beads and other fun stuff. Add stuffing and sew.

Artist Insider

Erin L. Shafkind

www.mustardworkstudio.com • Seattle, Washington

Do you have a helpful hint?

Wires are a great way to add arms, legs, whiskers, antennae, hairs or various other additions to a plush friend. Just be sure to warn any potential buyers (of these inclusions) if the plushie is for a child under the age of three.

Artist Insider

Mai Le

www.magpie.blogspot.com • San Francisco, California

Is this your full-time job? If not, what is?

*No. I work as an arts administrator at a museum; soon I'll no longer do that.
I'm not sure what my "real job" will be next.*

*Louis, Kayo
and
Sayo*

Friend

or

Foe

Artist Insider

Friend or Foe

www.incrediblythin.com/projects/look/stuffies • Pittsburgh, Pennsylvania

What's your favorite fabric?

Fabric that's been stashed away in some gramma's attic until being discovered and put out on the dollar table at the "estate sale." Our favorite is polyester— the kind that's so ridiculous you wonder what in the world would someone make with it besides a stuffed monster.

113

Boofyboof (Adam)

www.boofyboof.com • Seattle, Washington

What are your goals for your plush business?

A Boof on Mars by 2014.

Boofs

Pink Pirate Bunny,
Robot and
Ice Cream Bear

◉ Artist Insider ◉

Lisa Martin-Bowman (PixieGirl Art)
www.picturetrail.com/feyprincess • Woodbury, Tennessee

What's your favorite sewing machine?
A new Brother machine and a very old, early 1920s Singer.

Foxley Bagel

I love bagels. I love them so much that I always have one hidden in my tail pocket for later. Along with bagels, I hide secrets and maybe a boysenberry jam packet. I hate anyone who doesn't like bagels or the color orange. My best friend is a fish named Loxley Fin who can't eat wheat, so he sticks to seaweed and lichens. I secretly would love to eat Loxley on a bagel, but that secret will just have to stay in my tail for now.

Necessities
xxxxx xxxxx xxxx
¼ yard (23cm) orange wool or felt

white craft felt for face and cheeks

scrap of green felt for scarf

scrap of cotton fabric for heart

scrap of black felt for the nose

stuffing material

matching thread

black thread

fabric glue stick

pen for tracing

pins

needle

scissors

sewing machine (optional)

Artist Insider

Ashley Baker
www.be-adorn.com • Seattle, Washington

What's your favorite tool?
My rotary mat. Save your surfaces—get one of these! You'll thank me for it, and so will your table or floor or whatever.

1 Cut all pattern pieces

Trace and cut the pattern pieces (on page 137) as follows: 1 each of the nose, heart, face and tail pocket; 2 each of the tail, cheek puff and body; and 4 of the ear.

2 Create face

Stitch the white face piece to the front of the fox's head. Stitch the white cheek puffs on both sides. Using black thread, sew the eyes, snout and lips. You can imitate Foxley's or make up your own face.

3 Add heart, tail tip and nose

Stitch the heart to the fox's body. Stitch the white tip onto one piece of the tail. Stitch the two outer sides of the tip down; leave the third side open to form the tail pocket.

4 Attach ears

Take the 2 ear pieces and adhere them together with fabric glue to make a sturdier ear. Repeat for the next ear. Note: If you use a thick, sturdy fabric, you can skip this part. Take your 2 head pieces and put them with the right sides together with ears tucked inside, tips pointing down. Make sure to place the base of the ears level with where you're stitching the head closed. Pin in place and stitch a ⅛" (3mm) seam, leaving a 1½" (4cm) hole at the neck for stuffing. Note: To achieve more pointy cheeks, sew as close to the edge as possible, right at the two cheek edges, then bring it back to an ⅛" (3mm) for the rest of the face.

5 Stitch body and tail

Pin your 2 body pieces with the right sides together. Sew around the edges, leaving a 1½" (4cm) hole on the left lower side of the body for stuffing. (That's where the tail will go.) Place the right sides of the tail together and stitch up, leaving a hole at the end of the tail and extending about 1" (3cm) up the side of the tail for stuffing.

6 Turn, stuff and finish

Now turn all your pieces right-side out and stuff them. Blind stitch the head closed and attach it to the body by pinning it down and whipstitching them together. Blind stitch your tail and insert it in the open side of the body, tuck in your seams and blind stitch it all closed. Now wrap your scarf around his neck, and voilà!

You now own your own Foxley Bagel!

Artist Tips

❈ If you sew this by hand, be sure to use lots of tiny, tight stitches.

❈ Use less stuffing than possible to give the toy more of a soft, flexible feel.

❈ Try putting a piece of wire in his tail for bendable fun! (See how to add wire on page 110.)

Kroko,
From the Asylum

Artist Insider

Parapleusch
www.parapluesch.de • Hamburg, Germany

What's your favorite TV show?
I don't have a TV anymore. It was Ren & Stimpy.

118

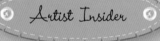

⊙ *Artist Insider* ⊙

Fiona Dalton
www.hopskipjump.typepad.com • Adelaide, Australia

What's your inspiration?

I'm fascinated with design from the 1920s through to the 1960s. Textiles, clothing, furniture and patterns from those times always draw me in. I studied social history at university for four years. So, items that might have a story behind them always hold a bit of mystery to me.

Esmerelda Monkey

Fuzz Puffs of Smoke and Fuzz Cigarettes

Artist Insider

Bink Creations

www.binkywinky.com • Seattle, Washington, and Tennessee

What's your favorite sandwich?

*Bloody Valentine: hummus, lettuce, jalapeño, sprouts,
habanero sauce and onion in a pita.*

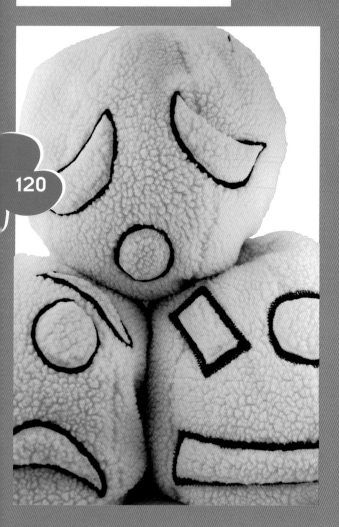

Jessica Sunshine Barnes

www.flickr.com/photos/misssockmonkey • Seattle, Washington

What's your dream job?

I think working with animals in some capacity would be amazing! I've always dreamt of working with chimpanzees or with dolphins—something crazy and exotic where you have to travel the open seas or traverse lush jungles.

Señor Squidly

121

Parskid

www.parskid.com • Seattle, Washington

What's your favorite extracurricular activity?
Either vandalism or drinking. They go pretty well together though.

Parsbat

Mama Doll, Mibala and Max Terrier

Speck, the Fuzzy Monster

I like to play soccer with the dust bunnies and dance with the lost socks. My favorite smell is lemon-scented furniture polish, mostly because it really freaks the dust bunnies out.

Necessities

thin, fuzzy yarn (weight 2 or 3)

thicker, more bulky yarn (weight 5 or 6)

18mm clip-in, stuffed-animal eyeballs

stuffing material

stitch marker

row counter

crochet hook US H/8 (5mm)

scissors

Artist Insider

Karyn Lane

www.karynlane.com • Portland, Oregon

Why do you do this?

These odd little creatures come into my head, and if I don't realize them in fibers, they just hang out in my psyche and taunt me all day (and night) long. So I do this for my sanity.

Make body

Slipknot, then chain 3 and slip stitch into the first chain, joining and making a circle.

R1: *2 sc into each chain*, repeat 3 times. (6 stitches)

Mark the end of row with a stitch marker.

R2: *2 sc into each sc*, repeat 6 times. (12 stitches)

(You should've ended up making the last stitch of this row in the marked stitch. Advance stitch marker to the end of your new row and continue to do this at the end of every row.)

R3: *1 sc in next sc, 2 sc in following sc* repeat 6 times. (18 stitches)

R4: *1 sc in next 2 scs, 2 sc in 3rd sc* repeat 6 times. (24 stitches)

R5: *1 sc in next 3 scs, 2 sc in 4th sc* repeat 6 times. (30 stitches)

R6–11: sc in each sc (30 stitches)

Apply eyeballs

I left the leading yarn for hair, so you could use that spot as a reference for your eye placement.

R12: *1 sc then decrease, making next 2 sc just one* repeat 10 times. (20 stitches)

R13: *1 sc then decrease making next 2 sc just one* repeat 6 times. Then 1 sc in each of the last 2 sc stitches to complete the row. (14 stitches)

R14: *1 sc then decrease making next 2 sc from the previous row just one* repeat 4 times. Then 1 sc in each of the last 2 sc stitches to complete the row. (10 stitches)

Stuff and finish

Row15: *decrease for every stitch now making every 2 sc from the previous row just one* repeat 5 times (5 stitches)

Row16: *decrease for every stitch, making every 2 sc from the previous row just one* repeat 2 times. Then 1 sc in sc stitch to complete the row. (3 stitches)

R17: *decrease for every stitch, making every 2 sc from the previous row just one* repeat 1 time. Finish off monster ball by pulling the remaining thread into the ball so you can no longer see it.

Make arms

Attach the yarn to a hook with a slipknot. Insert the hook into the monster from where you want the arms to sprout. Attach the yarn to that spot with a slip stitch. Chain as many stitches as you want your arms to be long—I did 20. These guys are great for tying around another gift. Though, if you want to do that, make your arms as long as you need to tie (or safety pin) around your wine bottle or keys to the new Karmann Ghia you bought for that special someone.

Create fingers

Trace your way back 3 stitches by skipping the first stitch; then 1 sl in each of next 3 chains. Next finger: chain 4, skip the first stitch, then 1 sl in each of next 3 chains. Repeat for as many fingers as you want your little guy to have.

Complete arm

Sl st in each of the chain stitches back to the body, tie off, and hide the leftover yarn tails. Repeat this process for as many arms as you want your little guy to have, I stuck with two, but your little guy would be much more helpful if he had 5 or 6 arms, don't you think?

Mr. Pickles
Gang

Artist Insider

Mr. Pickles
www.mrpickles.com • Columbus, Ohio

What's your next vacation destination?
As a group, we'll most likely be going to Hawaii in the winter.
Ooka laka haka! More poi, please!

Mr. Fudge Pop,
I Luv Your
Guts Monster and
Cookie Bag

Artist Insider

Denise Cozzitorto
www.heydayfashion.com • Sacramento, California

Who is your favorite plush artist?
Heidi Kenney (You can see Heidi's work on page 72.)

12PUNT3 (www.12punt3.nl,) a.k.a. Marianne Roosa, is a graphic designer/illustrator from The Hague, Netherlands. She created her first Oneye character in 2005. They're now sold around the world and seen in international plush art shows. **Arbito** (www.arbito.com) is a Washington native who spends most of his time creating artwork made of paint and wood. His hippie characters and politically confused slogans are always recognizable and funny. **Max Badger** (www.maxbadger. com) is a twenty-one-year-old artist living in Seattle. He enjoys music, art, movies, quality people and great "lit'rature." **Ashley Baker** (www.ashleybaker.etsy.com) is an artist/designer living in Seattle with her fiancé and three cats. Ashley also creates textile bags, screenprints her drawings and develops cute toys. **Courtney Barnebey** (www.cbarnebey.com) is a game designer/illustrator from Seattle. He wanted to learn to sew and silkscreen. Creating a simple plush toy was a great way to combine the two. **Jessica Sunshine Barnes** (www.flickr.com/photos/misssockmonkey) lives in Seattle with her husband, two Chihuahuas and an age-defying cat. She also creates fun Web sites and games for kids and tweens. **BINK Creations** (www.binkywinky. com) was started in 2005 and has evolved to include a variety of products and designs. The goal of this project is storytelling through playful designs that have more to say than a simple first glance allows. **Bisbee Stitches** (www.bisbeestitches. com) originated from Mark Hundley's desire to create unique, handcrafted gifts for his niece and nephew. Every Stitch is accompanied by a handmade card telling some of its favorite things. **John Black** is a Seattle artist who's shown his work in the Northwest since 1992. He has an eclectic style in painting, plush and sculpture with influences that range from Salvador Dali to *Mad* Magazine and everything between. **Blackbird Fashion** (www.blackbirdfashion.com) was born in the late 1990s, although its seeds were planted many years earlier when Clarity Miller's mom helped her sew a leotard and tutu for her Cabbage Patch doll. **Blobby Farm** (www.blobbyfarm. com) was started by Maria Samuelson and Christopher Lynn in 2004 in Chicago. Maria has misplaced her graduate degree under piles and stacks of fabric. Christopher is trained in painting and drawing and now spends his days directing a contemporary art gallery. **Boofyboof** (www.boofyboof.com) was formed in Seattle in 2005. It's the art and craft collective of Adam G. and Kaela G. (their "G"s are different). Named after a word that was once synonymous with flatulence, "boof" now describes the beings they create and depict. **BridgeTroll** (www.bridgetroll.net) is the creation of Joslyn Sherry, who currently resides in New Mexico. She writes, knits, sews, bakes and makes plush—mostly while her two young children are sleeping. **BURD** (www.hellobabyburd.blogspot.com) is Lucy Marten, who shows her love of the earth, nature and animals through everything she creates. Her streamlined style translates into all that she does. **Anna Chambers** currently works in television animation at Cartoon Network as a background painter. Her plush have been featured in shows and magazines around the world. She recently finished directing her own animated short for Disney. **Cherry Tomato** (www. cherrytomato.typepad.com) lives in Seattle, Washington, with her husband and three cats. She comes from generations of women who've sewn, knitted, crocheted and engaged in all sorts of creative endeavors. Her first plush animal was a horrendous-looking kitty, but she learned a lot from the process. **Cockeyed Sock Monkey** (www. cockeyedsockmonkey.blogspot.com) was founded in 2005 by Adrienne Bourne. She started making sock monkeys as gifts for her family and friends and now sells them around the Seattle area. Each sock monkey is handmade and an original. **Lisa Congdon** (www.lisacongdon.com) is a mixed-media artist and illustrator from San Francisco who works in paper collage, screenprinting, ink, textiles and paint. She's been featured in *Bitch, Adorn, Country Living* and *ReadyMade* and on juxtapoz.com and design*sponge. **Denise Cozzitorto** (www.heydayfashion.com) just moved with her cartoonist husband to North Carolina. Her mother taught her the love of crafting, sewing and crochet. She started her online business in 2002. Her goal is to create items that are fun and functional. **Wendy Crabb** (www.greengirlart.com) is primarily a painter, but she also dabbles in softies, drawing and photography. Wendy's "characters" have distinct personalities. Wendy believes that if you look hard enough, you will find a story to tell. **Cutesypoo** (www.cutesypoo.blogspot.com) toys are handmade made by Jocelan Hillton—a workaholic in the animation business. She hopes to expand Cutesypoo in the future but will always keep things fun and, of course, cute! **Fiona Dalton** (www.hopskipjump.typepad.com) lives in Adelaide, Australia, with her husband and daughter. When she's not being a full-time mom, she's a part-time graphic designer and other-time crafter. **Corinne Dean** (www. nottoopink.etsy.com) likes things pink (but not too pink). She has a husband, a little daughter and a little dog. Her family has just moved and she's trying the stay-at-home-mom thing. She tries to spend all her free time making art, looking at art or at least making something! **Fawne DeRosia** (www. momentofstars.com) lives in a small town in Georgia with her husband and their daughter. She paints, crochets and makes linoleum block prints and cute stuffed animals. She collects postcards, takes photos with vintage cameras and creates zines and mini comics. **Beth Doherty** (www.gourmetamigurumi. com) planned to become rich and famous making detailed paintings inspired by the craftsmanship of Japanese wood blocks and the colors of pop art. Now she plans to do that

with yarn instead of paint. **Camilla Engman** (www. camillaengman.com) practiced her skills at the Dome Art School and the School of Design and Craft, Gothenburg University, where she acquired a Master of Fine Arts degree. Camilla has been commissioned by the *New York Times*, British Columbia Airlines and Walt Disney, to name but a few. **Amanda Etches-Johnson** (www.etches-johnson.com) is a librarian and loves it. She lives in Toronto with her husband and two cats. She likes to do things with yarn, needles, fabric, paint, paper, pens, buttons, ribbons, trim and thread. **Felt Friends** (www.feltfriends.com), a.k.a. Kelley Callicoat, got a passion for sewing things while pregnant with her daughter and hasn't stopped since. (Sadly for everyone, the cake baking was a phase.) She's been in many shows around the Northwest, and has plush creatures in several stores in the United States. **Friend or Foe** (www.incrediblythin.com/projects/look/ stuffies) creations are one-of-a-kind lovely and frightful handmade stuffies sewn together from vintage fabrics, found material and various clothing. Some are friends, some are foes. They're created in Pittsburgh with love. **Laura Faust** (www.milkywayandthegalaxygirls.com) has worked in the animation industry for nine years. She's worked on *The Powerpuff Girls* and now writes for *Foster's Home for Imaginary Friends*. Her greatest goal as an artist is to offer up to little girls images of girls and women as positive, self-affirming, active, individualistic, fun—and even a little edgy. **Abby Glassenberg** (www.whileshenaps.typepad. com) is a soft-toy artist and mother living in Wellesley, Massachusetts. While her young daughters nap, Abby sews handmade soft toys in her home studio using vintage and unique fabrics. Abby's toys have been exhibited at the Wellesley Public Library, Plush You and at the Morphe II show. **Ashley Goldberg** (www.kittygenius.com) resides in St. Louis, Missouri. She has loved arts, crafts, creatures and nature her entire life. The characters she creates, whether monsters or little girls, are simple, humorous, empathetic and a little bit pathetic. Over the years, her creatures have become decidedly more design-driven, but a part of her is still just drawing little friends to have. **Laura Granlund** (www.intimidnation.com), a Chicago-based artist, runs a small studio called Intimidnation. In 2003, she created her first "Mr. Beardsley," a bearded gnome-like monkey that wore a removable disguise. Now Mr. Beardsley has been making his way into collaborative plush art shows all around the country! **Lizette Greco**'s (www.lizettegreco.com) two children draw and provide Lizette and her husband the characters from which to create patterns and choose the fabrics for their softies. They use thrifted, vintage and recycled fabrics, and linen lint from industrial linen dryers to stuff and make toys that are environmentally friendly and one-of-a-kind. **Jenny Harada**'s mom taught her to sew when she was very wee, and she's been making stuff ever since. She makes toys and kid stuff much more than clothes and grown-up stuff. **House of Ingri** (www.houseofingri.com) is a little toy company based in Brooklyn. The dolls are crafted from Naugahyde vinyl and have hand-placed acrylic eyes and noses. **Jess Hutchison** (www.jesshutch.com) was born on Guam and now resides in San Francisco with her husband and her cat. Jess is inspired by vintage toys, Victorian popular culture, world's fairs and other toy artists. **David Huyck** (www.bunchofmonkeys.com) grew up in Chicago, one-half block from the schoolyard in one direction and the candy store in the other direction. The playground provided emotional and physical trauma that now serves as a fertile source of inspiration. The convenience store provided many childhood pleasures, such as Lik-M-Aid, Pop Rocks and root beer barrels. With Saturday morning cartoons, the *Muppet Show*, Ed Emberly how-to-draw books, Legos, *The Far Side*, *Calvin and Hobbes*, Atari and Nintendo, these psychological and high-fructose fuels mix to make a sticky goo at the heart of David's artwork. **Chad Jacobsen** is a plush artist from Seattle who fills his time since *Arrested Development* was cancelled writing biographical haikus:

Chad is a rad guy
He likes to sketch and doodle
He also eats food

Mandy Jouan (www.sappymoostree.com) designs silly, playful and, sometimes, crazy creations. She's best known for Buttons, the sock monkey of epic proportions (fifteen feet tall), magical magnetic bacon and Steve the Sock Monkey Zombie. **Heidi Kenney** is the creator of My Paper Crane, which tries to embody the thought of taking something simple and turning it into something amazing. **Serena Kuhl** tried toy making after having a few solo shows of soft sculpture. She found that having a sense of humor was more important than developing a conceptual premise. **La puce à l'agonie** (www.pucealagonie.com) is a plush artist from Montreal, Quebec. She created a pink cat named Minouchka in an attempt to share her inner self. Her work speaks about the loss of innocence and transforms the melancholy into pure bliss. **Sam Lamb** (www.samlamb.blogspot.com) knits, crochets, embroiders, cross-stitches, writes, doodles—anything to keep her hands busy. With a toddler, a husband and a full-time job, knitting is the perfect pastime. **Karyn Lane** worked as a bench jeweler for two years in New York. She moved to Portland, Oregon, in 2002 and is now in nursing school to support her family and artwork. She's not very good at following directions, so she makes up her own patterns even when she's trying to follow one. She was raised on B movies and loves monsters and anything sinister. **Mai Le** (www.magpie.blogspot.com) makes plush art toys from recycled fabrics and is inspired by film, nature, music and color. Currently she prefers using kimono, wool, cotton and (sometimes) leather. Her colorful one-of-a-kind creatures are constructed with care in her San Francisco apartment. **Le Merde** (www.lemerde.com) is Seattle-based husband-and-wife duo Mike and Michelle Kelly. Their work ranges from paintings and sculpture to hand-cast toys, plushies and tote bags. They draw inspiration from pop culture, including heavy-metal music and 1970s' cartoon characters.

littleoddforest (www.forestprints.com) was created by Lynda Lye. Her unbridled passion for pervasive creativity is infused throughout her line of handmade products, from brooches and bags to oh-so-huggable plush. Currently littleoddforest is silkscreened tops, quirky bags and accessories, lovable plush, home décor items and paper goods. **Longoland** is a creative powerhouse consisting of fifty to sixty longos packed into a small room looking for a reason. Along with commissioned work, Longoland provides creative consulting to businesses, artists and the military. Longoland's CEO Joshua is also a motivational speaker. **Look What I Can Do** (www. plush-a-holic.blogspot.com) is Dawn Ramerman, a stay-at-home mom who likes to sew, take photographs, make clothing for her daughter and collage. **Madame Edgar**, **Inc.** hails from Quebec and has been inspired by an eclectic mix of artists, including Jim Henson, Tim Burton and Martha Stewart. **Ariana Marinelli** (www.furrybanana.blogspot.com) stitches dreamy stuffed landscapes from a variety of materials. She is inspired by flowering trees, vintage toys, the films of Hayao Miyazaki, Icelandic pop music and her earless cat. She lives in Portland, Oregon. **Lisa Martin-Bowman** (www.picturetrail. com/feyprincess) is a creator of mixed-media art, photographs, artist trading cards, altered books and plush toys. **Moki** (www. thegoodneighbor.blogspot.com) is a professional photographer trying to balance a job, motherhood and her insane obsession with anything art related. **Emerald Mosley** (www.goldtop. org) makes stuff. Sometimes it's Web sites, sometimes it's felt birds and snails. Other times it's illustrations or badges. Or cakes. **Mr. Pickles** is the telepathic brother-sister team of Jack and Rita Volpi. They came up for the idea for Mr. Pickles on the same day about four hundred miles apart. Jack thought, "He's a pickle that wears glasses." Rita thought, "Yes, and we'll have an awesome Web site and sell rad stuff." Then Jack thought, "I hope your husband can sew." And that's the totally true story of how they started their company. **Mucho**, a.k.a. Pamela Yearby, lives happily in Seattle. She likes cute kitties, breakfast foods, cigarettes and petite cheri. She's currently obsessed with *The Kinks Are the Village Green Preservation Society*. Crafting is her way of staving off boredom. **Chrystal Myers** (www. plumpkin.ca) lives in sunny British Columbia with her daughter and husband, who are her greatest artistic inspirations. She splits her time working as a graphic designer and being a stay-at-home mom. She finds great fulfillment in creating unique and thoughtful crafts for her friends and family. **Ryan Myers**'s playful and somber paintings, plush dolls and vinyl toys grew out of an obsession with Pee Wee Herman and the bad children from *Willy Wonka and the Chocolate Factory*. His works reflect an interruptive view into a sullen, mannequinesque world where sadness is masked in pinks, greens and blues. He currently lives and paints with his wife, dog and a spiteful lovebird. **onegirl designwrks** (www.onegirldesignwrks. blogspot.com) equals Canadian hands designing and creating in Melbourne, thrift shopping, glossy magazines, roasted almonds, green tea, muted colors, crisp linen, wool felt, organic pottery, tiny seashells, bonsai, woodcut prints, chamomile, the patterns of wood, scandinavian design, japanese craft books, line drawings, dark chocolate and hand dying fabric. **Parapluesch** (www. parapluesch.de) is from the mind of Martin Kittsteiner, the creator of the online game The Asylum (Psychiatric Clinic for Abused Cuddly Toys). Visit the Asylum (www.parapluesch. de) and you can fill in for Dr. Kindermann, the clinic's director, and treat four mentally disturbed soft-toy patients. **Parskid** experiments with paint, plush and digital mediums. His work has been exhibited in many cities in the United States. When he's not curled up in his dark underground lair he enjoys dripping marsh ink, spraying rusto paint and playing by the tracks. **Marilyn Patrizio** (www.mpatrizio.com) has an extensive striped knee-high sock collection that anyone would envy. She enjoys collecting anything Japanese, polka-dot, baby blue, plastic or stainless steel. **Magdalena Pereyra** is a Melbourne, Australia-based textile artist. She designs and produces bags called "magsBags," knitted scarves and stuffed dolls called "Maggagles." Stuffed toys are where her darkness, quirkiness and cheekiness all come out. Each of her toys is handmade and painted. **Sonja Peterson** mainly paints and makes ceramics, plush critters and mobiles. She's inspired by her little boy. She designed a line of hats with small ears for kids and adults, which she makes from recycled sweaters. **Pied Nu** (www.lepiednu.com) is a plush artist who hails from Tokyo, but now calls Seattle home. Here she makes her plush creations along with purses, mittens, scarves, tote bags and more. **Plushood** consists of Shlomi Schillinger and Tamar Moshkovitz. Shlomi has worked as a freelance art director and set designer for commercials, TV shows, fashion, catalogues and magazines. Tamar's animated short "Joined" was screened in festivals in Israel and the world and received an honorable mention at the Tenth International Student Film Festival—Tel Aviv. **pyglet whispers** (www.pygletwhispers.etsy.com) is Dani Choate, a stay-at-home mom who creates a variety of plush and other goods out of a sheer compulsion to maintain her sanity. She spends her days with a cheeky toddler while she waits for her next little bundle of joyful insanity to arrive. **Chandra Rankin** (www.littlefiends.com) is the creator of naughty monsters, Little Fiends. She loves the colors orange and purple, orchids, the combination of peanut butter and chocolate and making her son smile. On her list of things she would love to do: sleep in, visit Japan and create a travel book of the Little Fiends' world adventures. **Kristen Rask** (www.schmancytoys.com) is the owner of Schmancy and the curator of Plush You! She likes coffee, but still loves iced tea. She loves her cats and really loves craft nights with friends and wine. She makes all kinds of stuff, including button rings, plush pins, and sewn items. **Aimee Ray** (www.dreamfollow.com) has been an artist all her life. She has a head full of ideas and is constantly working on something, from painting and illustration to sewing stuffed animals and other oddities. She's also written a book of embroidery patterns and projects. **Ana Paula Rimoli** was born in Montevideo, Uruguay, a country full of great artists that inspired her. Her dream as a little girl was to have a stand in Tristan Narvaja's street market where she could sell the toys, hats and scarves she couldn't stop making. Once she found Etsy, she opened shop and quit her boring, depressing office job. **Natascha S. Rosenberg** (www.natascharosenberg.com) has been working as a freelance illustrator since 1998, illustrating children's fiction and educational books by other authors, designing postcards and Web sites as well as producing personal works with a variety of techniques and materials ranging from pop-ups and flaps to textiles and screen printing. **Ivy Russell** (www.pinned.blah.net) makes things to keep her sane. She sells them so she can make more things. **Samantha Salway** created Plump Pudding to provide exclusive handcrafted accessories for you and your home. All things vintage inspire her to create the Plump Pudding range. Warm, cuddly childhood memories have led to the introduction of soft woollen characters. **Toi Sennhauser** (www.toisennhauser.com) was born in Bangkok, Thailand. When not making food-influenced performance art and soft sculpture she spends time with her baby daughter. She now lives in Seattle. **Debbie Severtson** (www.butteredparsnips.etsy.com) lives in Richmond, Virginia, with her husband and youngest son. When she's lucky, things settle down and needle and thread come together, and she makes something that others like! **Sewdorky**—Maker of Fine Felted Handstitched Donuts and School of Dentistry (www.sewdorky.com) is headquartered in the corner of a cozy little bedroom in scenic West Seattle. Sewdorky consists of, well, mostly one person and some friends, and has been creating plush objects and sending them around the globe for several years. That one person (Stuart) has a lovely wife and a brand new baby boy, who is awesome. **Sewing Stars** (www.sewingstars.com) is run by Teresa Levy of Providence, Rhode Island. In her studio all sorts of creations spring to life—from unique plush dolls to using her artwork to create zipper pouches and stationery products. All her creations are inspired by Japanese art, vintage design, and intense color combinations. **Erin L. Shafkind** (www.mustardworkstudio.com) divides her time between teaching art, collecting strange items and taking pictures. Her best friend and muse is a doll named Little Roy. She collects plush dolls, state quarters and kumquat seeds. She hates the taste of yellow mustard but loves the concept. **Shawnimals** started in 2001 by Shawnimals Shawn after his wife became disenchanted with the droves of sketchbooks he had lying around. "Why not make plush versions of these simple-shaped characters?" Soon after dozens of plush creatures were born. Shawnimals continues to grow in popularity, receiving press in *Entertainment Weekly, New York Times, Chicago Sun-Times,* MTV.com and many others. **Sooz** (www.soozs.blogspot.com) is a craftsperson working in Melbourne, Australia. With the birth of her first child, Sooz became interested in toys and other objects for children. Her toys center on natural materials and opportunities for imaginative and interactive play. **Andrea L. Stern** (www.andibeads.blogspot.com) is well-known for her detailed beadwork and art quilts. Making plush creatures allows her to express a more whimsical side and use the skills she's acquired in making her other artwork. She hopes to collaborate with her father in the future on a series of creatures based on his drawings. **Blair Stocker** (www.blairpeter.typepad.com) lives in the Pacific Northwest with her husband and two children. She's inspired by many things in life: making a great meal, vintage children's books, postage stamps, her kids sleeping on homemade bed linens, the perfect cup of coffee and Denyse Schmidt quilt designs. **Suicide Kittens** (www.suicidekittens.com) is a plush artist from New York City. The goal of Suicide Kittens is "to bring you conventional and individual products, recycling dead products when we can to make new ones. Hot." **tsai-fi** (www.tsai-fi.com/thelink.html) has an obsession with creating cute characters that have a little evil streak deep inside. These characters center around

humorous issues that adult collectors can easily relate to, such as excessive drinking and poking fun at nerdy behavior. **Michelle Valigura** (www.thegirlsproductions.com) is one half of The Girls Productions with Amanda Visell. They have worked in stop-motion animation as fabricators and sculptors for the past six years. **Berber Vos** (www.kisskus.typepad.com), is a Dutch mom who is always thinking up new things to sew. **P. Williams** (www.pwilliamsart.com) started noticing things in the suburban culture of his native Orange County, California: the architecture, the street grids and the lives of the people who lived there. These things began to appear in his paintings, which grew into installations and then became plush sculptures that are now a new system of myths echoing the sprawling miles of track homes and master planned communities. **Woollyhoodwinks'** creator Jeff Root grew up in western New York in a very creative home, where television was discouraged and fun projects were offered instead. Jeff and his brother would sew their own beanbags and worked their way up to crude stuffed animals. Jeff was encouraged by friends to continue creating plush creatures. Friend Scott Runcorn joined the creative process with his masterful animation abilities, and the Woollyhoodwinks were born in 2004. **Karin Yamagiwa Madan** (www.stumpytown.com) is a maker of "things and stuff." Working with a variety of media that includes markers, paint, clay, fabric and Shrinky Dinks, she creates memorable and endearing artwork exploring themes of innocence, loss, love, kinship and alienation. Her some-of-a-kind artworks of Stumpytown are based on memories of childhood and traits of friends and loved ones. **Jou Ling Yee**, as a wee little one, fooled around with her grandmother's crochet projects, playing with needle and yarn. In 2005, she created Amigurumi Kingdom, her online store, and began selling her own creations. Amigurumi (Japanese style crochet) is perfect for her, as she is obsessed with cute things and loves to craft. She works in color production for the fashion industry.

Patterns

B
Body
cut 2 from a plaid, houndstooth or herringbone fabric

A
Head
cut 2 from a solid color fabric

C
Leg
cut 2 from a solid color fabric

Scale 200%

Woollyhoodwinks, page 20

Scale 145%

Sasha the Whale Pin, page 68

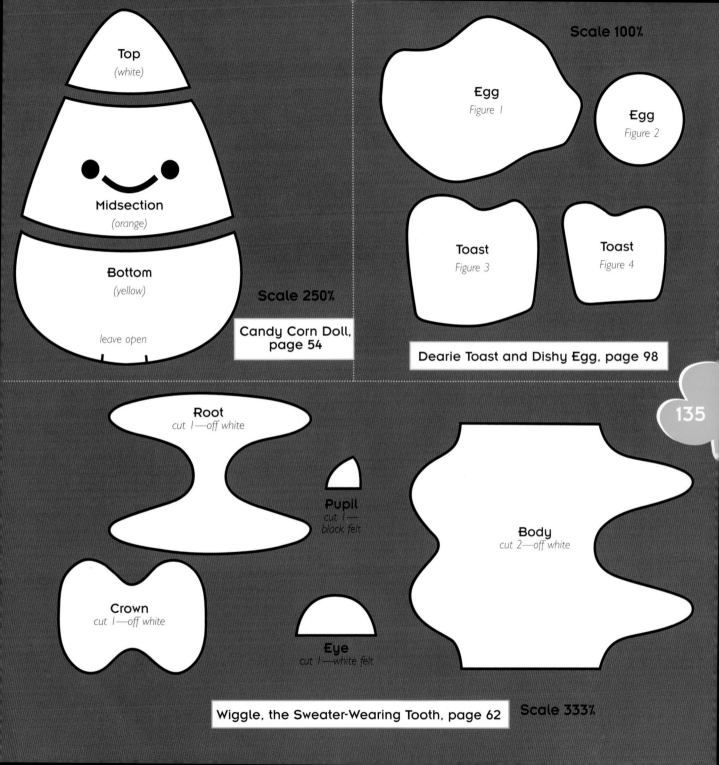

Top
(white)

Midsection
(orange)

Bottom
(yellow)

leave open

Scale 250%

Candy Corn Doll,
page 54

Scale 100%

Egg
Figure 1

Egg
Figure 2

Toast
Figure 3

Toast
Figure 4

Dearie Toast and Dishy Egg, page 98

135

Root
cut 1—off white

Pupil
*cut 1—
black felt*

Body
cut 2—off white

Crown
cut 1—off white

Eye
cut 1—white felt

Wiggle, the Sweater-Wearing Tooth, page 62

Scale 333%

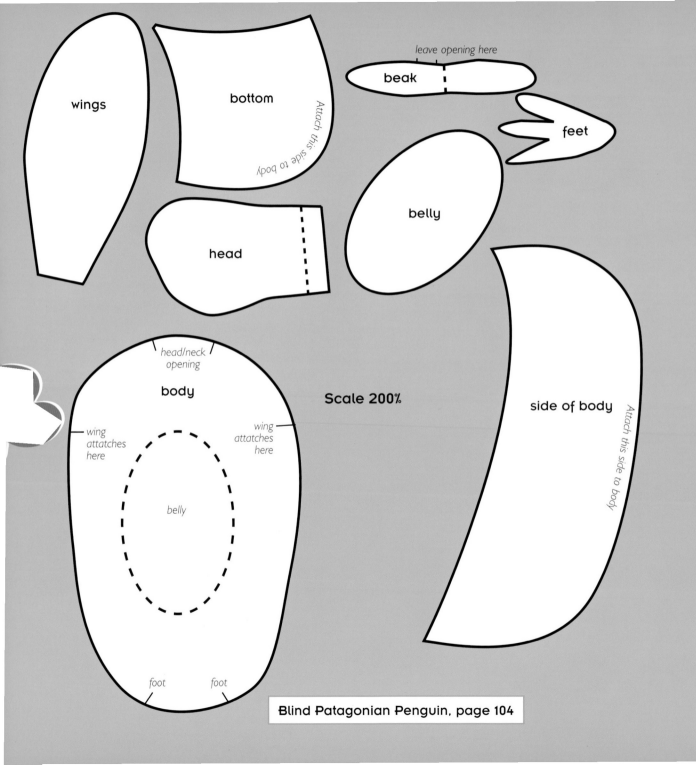

wings

bottom

Attach this side to body

leave opening here

beak

feet

head

belly

head/neck
opening

body

Scale 200%

side of body

Attach this side to body

wing
attaches
here

wing
attatches
here

belly

foot *foot*

Blind Patagonian Penguin, page 104

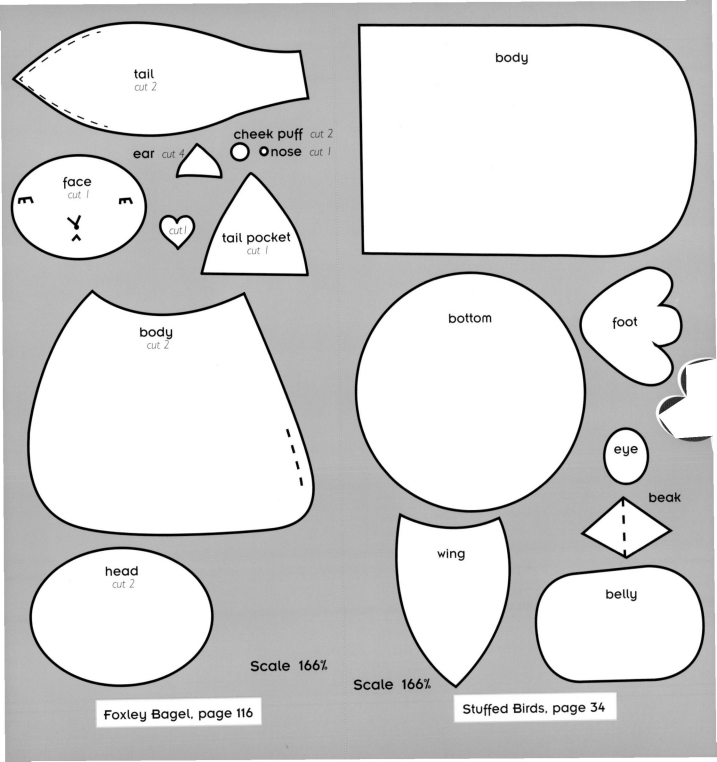

tail
cut 2

cheek puff *cut 2*
nose *cut 1*

ear *cut 4*

body

face
cut 1

cut 1

tail pocket
cut 1

body
cut 2

bottom

foot

eye

beak

wing

belly

head
cut 2

Scale 166%

Scale 166%

Foxley Bagel, page 116

Stuffed Birds, page 34

Scale 200%

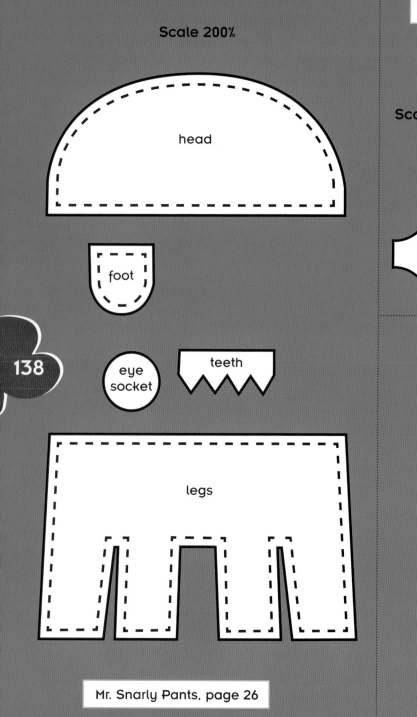

head

foot

eye socket

teeth

legs

Mr. Snarly Pants, page 26

Felt Snails, page 48

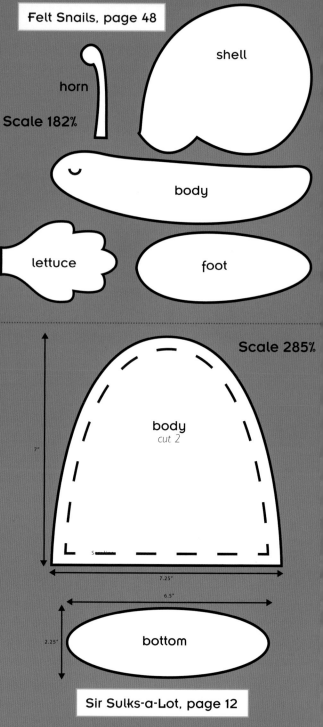

shell

horn

Scale 182%

body

lettuce

foot

Scale 285%

body
cut 2

7"

7.25"

6.5"

2.25"

bottom

Sir Sulks-a-Lot, page 12

Scale 148%

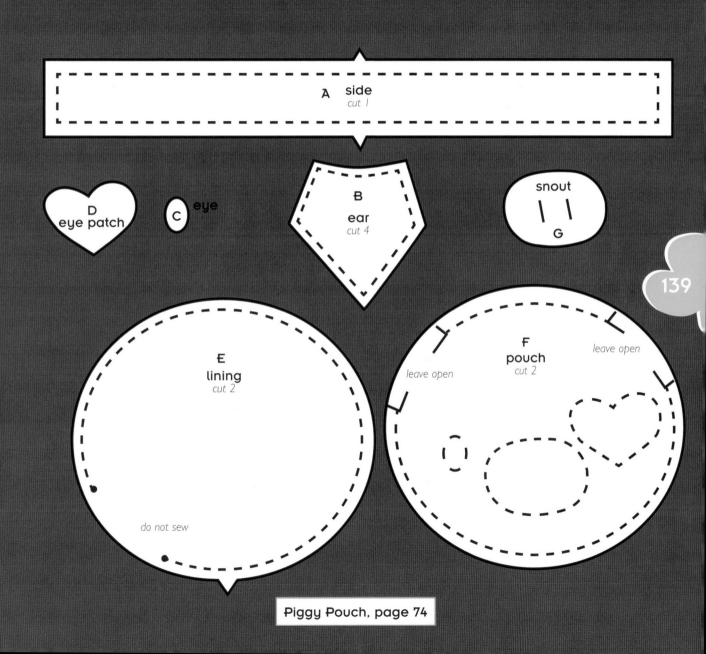

A side
cut 1

D
eye patch

C eye

B
ear
cut 4

snout

G

139

E
lining
cut 2

do not sew

F
pouch
cut 2

leave open

leave open

Piggy Pouch, page 74

Reprodepot Fabrics

Reprodepot Fabrics is popular among the craft community for cool fabrics, trim and other supplies.
www.reprodepotfabrics.com

Stitches

Seattle's Stitches is an awesome little shop full of fun fabrics and notions. The owner, Amy, is really nice and always willing to help with your questions. Sewing classes and machines are available, too!
www.stitchesseattle.com,
711 East Pike Street, Seattle, Washington

Purl

Purl.com is crafting Shangri-la: a beautiful and user-friendly Web site with tons of materials including books and patterns, fabric, yarn and notions. If you're lucky enough to live in New York City, you can even go there in person. Either way, have a look; it's just so dang pretty.
www.purlsoho.com/purl
137 Sullivan Street, New York City, New York

Kitty-Craft Japanese Zakka & Craft Shop

I am a goner for anything cute. When Abby Glassenberg directed me to this site, I had a hard time leaving. My wallet shall soon be empty, for this is a temple of all things sweet and lovely. It sort of makes me want to cry. If you fancy the cute you will love the Kitty-Craft.
www.kitty-craft.com

Superbuzzy

Superbuzzy is a distinctly adorable fabric and notion store. If you leave this place empty-handed either you deserve a trophy for your exemplary restraint or you have a black, black heart.
www.superbuzzy.com

SCRAP

SCRAP is a creative reuse center, store and workshop space. It helps to reduce the amount of waste going to crowded landfills. Each time I read about SCRAP on Lisa Congdon's blog, I want to hop on a plane and go there. Mai Le sent this write-up: "A few days ago I went to SCRAP. I had been before many years ago, but it's out of the way (off Evans, near Bayshore). Being the pedestrian and Muni person that I am, the distance is daunting. With the use of CW's van and the purpose of dropping off my unneeded-but-in-good-condition art supplies, I finally made a return visit. If you're a crafter or artist of any sort, it's a veritable wonderland of supplies. I could spend hours there dreaming of the projects I could complete with materials salvaged from the warehouse. Instead I reigned in my hoarding tendencies and walked away with buttons, three pieces of tapestry samples, thread and an embroidery frame for needlework!" Don't you want to go right now?
www.scrap-sf.org
801 Toland Street, San Francisco, California

Cia's Palette

Cia's has a beautiful selection of cotton fabric—from designer and Japanese to novelty and reproduction items. The fantastic selection is perfect for many kinds of projects.
www.ciaspalette.com/index.html

CR's Craft

CR's is an online store for dolls and bears, but you can use the supplies for plushies. CR's is tops for eyeballs, noses, mouths, stuffing and so much more. A win-win-win.
www.crscraft.com

Cartwright

Adding that special touch is the superfun part, giving more personality to your work. Beth Doherty should have a glue gun named for her in honor of all the small detailing she does. She shops here and so should you.
www.ccartwright.com

The obvious but not to be forgotten:
Etsy

Etsy is the best thing to happen to us in a long time. Full of cool finds that range from art and pillows to amigurumi and supplies! Don't forget that you can get your crafty supplies at Etsy too! We love Etsy, and so should you.
www.etsy.com

eBay

As much as eBay can be a pain (especially for the gambler in you…me…whatever), you can't deny the fact that there are some great finds. And when you get it, you feel like you hit the jackpot. Good luck bidding!
www.ebay.com

Thrift stores

To me, this seems the most obvious…but should not go without mentioning. If you have the patience, there's always something to be found at your local thrift store. I've looked for fabric in the bedding section, the baby clothes, the vintage section, etc. I do like to support my local thrift stores that give something back to the community. I always go to those stores first, as I know they actually do something good with their money. Either way, thrift-store shopping is fun and economical. With thrift stores there's no excuse to not craft.

Check out these fun other North Light Books!

Get Real Greetings
Edited by Jessica Strawser

The 70+ fresh, contemporary card designs in *Get Real Greetings* feature unsentimental sentiments for celebrating the sorts of occasions that don't get their own sections in greeting card stores. Make these cards to send to friends for the things that happen between holidays and birthdays: engagements and break-ups, bad job interviews and promotions, PMS and hot flashes—even divorces and speeding tickets. This book features instructions for creative cards, as well as bonus sidebars with alternate sentiments to help you say what you really mean.

ISBN-10: 1-60061-001-3
ISBN-13: 978-1-60061-001-1
paperback
112 pages
Z0990

Mr. Funky's Super Crochet Wonderful
By Narumi Ogawa

Mr. Funky's Super Crochet Wonderful is filled with 25 supercute crochet patterns for adorable Japanese-style stuffed animals and accessories. You'll find candy-color elephants, panda bears, kitty cats, hamsters and even a snake, plus fashionable hats, armwarmers and purses for girls of all ages. Each pattern features instructions as well as traditional amigurumi diagrams.

ISBN 10: 1-58180-966-2
ISBN 13: 978-1-58180-966-4
paperback
96 pages
Z0697

Knitted Toys
By Zoë Mellor

From a cute chick and a curly-haired doll to colorful mice and a patchwork tortoise, here you will find 25 unique designs for newborns to teens. Try knitting the colorful Stripy Ball for little ones to play with, or Goldilocks and the Three Bears Finger Puppets for older children to enjoy. The Shiny Robot has real retro charm while the Slithery Snake can even double up as a draught excluder!
With toys ranging from quick and easy to more complex designs, there's something for every child and every knitter.

ISBN-10: 1-58180-900-X
ISBN-13: 978-1-58180-900-8
paperback
144 pages
Z0311

These books and other fine North Light titles are available at your local craft retailer, bookstore or from online suppliers.